The Girls' Car Handbook

Everything You Need to Know about Life on the Road

MARIA McCARTHY

POCKET
BOOKS

LONDON • SYDNEY • NEW YORK • TORONTO

First published in Great Britain by Pocket Books, 2009
An imprint of Simon & Schuster UK Ltd
A CBS COMPANY

1 3 5 7 9 10 8 6 4 2

Simon & Schuster UK Ltd
1st Floor
222 Gray's Inn Road
London WC1X 8HB

www.simonandschuster.co.uk

Simon & Schuster Australia
Sydney

A CIP catalogue record for this book is
available from the British Library.

Illustrations by Kat Heyes

ISBN: 978-1-84739-215-2

Typeset by M Rules

Printed by CPI Cox & Wyman, Reading, Berkhire RG1 8EX

Contents

Acknowledgements

I'm very grateful to everyone who has helped during the research and writing of *The Girls' Car Handbook*.

I'm indebted to Dr Peter Russell, Professor of Road Safety at the Driver Education Research Foundation, driving consultant Kathy Higgins, motoring journalists Chris Pickering and Brian Taylor, and London taxi driver Richard Potter of Dial-a-Cab's *Call Sign* magazine, London bus depot manager Russ Nicol and Annette Gamble of www.2pass.co.uk, whose knowledgeable feedback has helped tremendously.

Other expert advisers have included Vanessa Guyll, technical specialist at the AA and top AA breakdown patrolman Adam Ashmore, motor mechanic Louise A'Barrow, Steph Savill of Foxy Lady Drivers, John Proctor of the Society of Motor Manufacturers and Traders, Mark Cornwall of Car Parts Direct, Steve Fowler of *What Car?* magazine, Alex Jenner-Fust of www.evecars.com, Hannah Dudek at Halfords, David Gerrans of Warranty Direct, David Evans, motoring specialist at Which?, Tony Bosworth of Friends of the Earth, driving instructor Chris Pope, parenting expert Patricia Carswell, Ruthie Collier-Large of www.me-mo.co.uk, Raymond Catchpole of the Feng Shui Society, Julie Bedford at The Blue Cross and David McDowell, veterinary expert at the RSPCA, Malcolm Tarling of the Association of British Insurers, Nigel Bartran of Norwich Union and Niki Bolton of Sheilas' Wheels. Thank you all so much for your help.

Amanda Preston has been a fantastic agent, wise and supportive throughout – many thanks to her and everyone else at Luigi Bonomi Associates. I'm also most grateful to Katherine Stanton for her editing and Kat Heyes for her wonderful illustrations.

A huge thank-you is due to the friends who shared their driving experiences and tips with such honesty and humour – Philippa, Rebecca, Juliette, Anna, Laura, Jackie, Rene, Kate, Sandra, Imogen, Helen, Ruby, Liz, Shelley, Rosy, Margaret, Evelyn, Fiona, Zoe, Edgar, Wendy and Adrian, members of the www.2pass.co.uk forum and all the girls at Journobiz. And as always I owe very special thanks to Stuart for his die-hard petrolhead advice and contributions.

Please do check out my website www.mariamccarthy.co.uk for useful driving links.

Chapter 1

Getting up to Speed

It's wonderful having a car – there's the freedom of being able to jump in and drive to see family and friends at a moment's notice, fill the boot with your supermarket shop rather than having to haul it home on the bus and take off to the beach on a sunny day.

But there are hassles too. Such as the fear of being ripped off by car salesmen and dodgy garages. Or the nagging feeling that you don't know enough (or indeed, anything at all) about what goes on under the bonnet and that one day your car might seize up and die because you haven't been sufficiently diligent when it comes to topping up some obscure fluid.

The stock answer to these problems tends to be that girls who don't feel confident when it comes to dealing with the motor trade and to whom doing the grease-monkey thing doesn't come naturally should turn to their nearest bloke – whether that's their dad, partner or a friend – for support. But there are flaws in this strategy. For starters, many of us like to be as independent as possible. And second, not all of us have vast quantities of car-savvy men in our lives that we can draw on at a moment's notice. You might be single, may not have any male family members living nearby and your bloke-mates might be of the metrosexual variety who are great when it comes to finding a companion for arty films but sadly lacking when it comes to anything grimy and mechanical.

In the past when I've dealt with a garage I've always taken my dad along as I reckon he's less likely to get patronized or leered at. But now he and my mum are retiring to Spain and he won't be able to come over whenever I need him. I haven't got a clue how I'm going to cope! Laura, 24

The car I have at present was bought new from a dealership four years ago when I still had a husband. It's going to have to last forever, largely because I have no intention of braving car showrooms, oily salesmen and strange blokes on the end of private-sale newspaper ads by myself. My plan at the moment is to enter every 'win a new car' competition I can find. Julia, 55

I don't know how to do those checks or pump up my tyres so I have to ask my husband. But he's always busy and I have to go on at him a bit before he gets round to it – it's really annoying and makes me feel like some awful stereotype of the sort of wife who's always nagging her husband to put up shelves. Katie, 32

Most of the current motoring TV programmes, newspaper supplements and books don't really address these issues. *Top Gear* is great if you want to compare the respective merits of Porsches, Lamborghinis and Ferraris, but less helpful if you're looking to buy a second-hand Nissan Micra. Mainstream motoring books offer useful advice on changing your brake pads, but blithely assume you'll already know how to top up the windscreen-washer fluid.

The Girls' Car Handbook takes a completely fresh and female-friendly approach, providing information and advice from both male and female motoring experts to help you tackle any driving challenge with confidence and style. It will help you:

- ⊕ Haggle with dealers in car showrooms and come out on top.
- ⊕ Find a garage you can trust.
- ⊕ Carry out the essential checks to keep your car running smoothly.

- ☻ Cope with driving disasters such as breakdowns and accidents.
- ☻ Stay sane on the school run.
- ☻ Get real about money and your motor – find out what your car is really costing you to run, and how to get the best possible deal on everything from fuel to insurance.
- ☻ Understand greener motoring – if you're one of the increasing number of girls who needs to run a car but still wants to keep her carbon footprint as light as possible, you'll have the options explained clearly and in a way that doesn't leave you feeling like you've accidentally wandered into an A-level Chemistry lecture.

And of course, *The Girls' Car Handbook* will help you get the maximum possible fun out of your driving life, with tips for music on the move, feng-shui-ing your car, and driving with the top down while still keeping your hair looking great.

Car culture

When you don't know much about cars, it's easy to find the whole subject completely bewildering. This isn't helped by the fact that most people involved in the world of motoring seem to talk a different language. Mechanics will warn you of problems with the crankshaft or carburettor. Car salesmen will hold forth about how a particular model has 'excellent residuals' and expect you to be impressed. Even the private sales adverts in local newspapers seem to be written in an impenetrable code, and are packed with cars described as having FDSH and RCL (that's full dealer service history and remote central locking, by the way).

Everyone knows that in lonely-hearts ads GSOH translates as 'good sense of humour' – and initially it can feel as though venturing into the motoring milieu means you're going to need one. But it really needn't be that bad – and over time you may even find the experience enjoyable. It can be helpful to see it as going to a foreign country. Making the effort to learn some of the language and make friends among the locals will make your trips so much more enjoyable.

Many girls will only be interested in flying visits – all you want is to do what's necessary to keep yourself on the road and not get ripped off in the process. Others might decide they want to spend more time there. This certainly isn't the sort of book which is going to push doing your own repairs and imply that you're letting the Suffragettes down if you're not prepared to get your hands dirty and learn to change your own spark plugs. It's got a more realistic approach than that, and accepts that for many of us a car is primarily a metal box for getting about conveniently and safely. And that while we might yearn for a nippy sports car or a VW camper van, what we're after is the fun aspect of driving a vehicle with a distinctive personality rather than an overwhelming urge to learn about how its particular sprockets work. But if you find you get into it, that's fantastic! Women are sadly under-represented when it comes to anything to do with cars, and it would be great to have some more of you on board.

If you would like to improve your driving skills then consider taking an advanced driving course. RoSPA (Royal Society for the Prevention of Accidents) and IAM (Institute of Advanced Motorists) both run courses that are very good value for money and where you'll be met with a warm welcome. Rally driving is fast and furious and if you're itching to release your inner Daisy Duke, it can be a fun hobby. Or if you just fancy having a go at driving vehicles as diverse as a double-decker bus or a fire engine then check out the Marie Curie Ladies' Driving Challenge at www.mariecurie.org.uk. These are charity events which ask participants to raise a certain amount in sponsorship and in return gives them the chance to have the sort of driving experiences that wouldn't normally come their way!

Once you feel confident doing basic checks and repairs, you might find that you'd like to take things a step further and learn how to service and do more advanced repairs on your car. Car maintenance classes are held via the adult education service in many areas and are a worthwhile investment for teaching you techniques and giving you confidence. And if you're a single girl they also double as a classic strategy for meeting men.

There aren't many positive role models for women working in the motor trade (teenage motor mechanic Charlene, played by Kylie Minogue in distant but fondly remembered episodes of *Neighbours*, almost makes the grade, but unfortunately is let down by that dreadful perm). But if you'd like a career as a mechanic or in another area such as car sales, don't be put off by the current state of affairs – things really are changing, and women are increasingly making inroads into areas previously seen as irredeemably blokeish and becoming successful and respected – maybe you could be one of them?

Finding out more

Hopefully, *The Girls' Car Handbook* will provide you with a good basic grounding in everything related to your little motor.

But don't let it stop there – see yourself as being on a learning curve. Gathering bits and bobs of car-related knowledge here and there will help you feel more confident and also mean that when you find yourself in a crisis situation – stuck by the roadside with a flat tyre, for example – you'll feel calmer as you'll have more of an idea of what to do.

One area in which it's particularly good (and indeed fun) to do research is about buying your next car. Whether you love your current car or view it with mistrust as an unreliable money-drain, the fact is there's no way of knowing when it might be involved in an accident or indeed just conk out and have to go to the Great Car Park in the Sky. If you need a car for work or ferrying children then you'll need to replace it sharpish, and having to make decisions and do research in a hurry leaves you more vulnerable to making a costly mistake. So get into the habit of reading car reviews in the paper, flicking through the newspaper small ads and just developing an idea of what's out there in your price range. Or indeed fantasizing about which particular dream car you'd buy if you won the lottery. *What Car?* magazine is a particularly helpful guide, and presents information in a way that's clear and accessible even if you're not a petrolhead.

Reading through the motoring supplements in the paper can be useful too – don't be put off by the fact that some of the features will be about incomprehensible subjects such as torque. There's often useful information in them about more everyday stuff such as winter motoring or getting a better deal on car insurance.

Then of course there's the internet – how did we ever manage without it? Motoring sites on the web are often linked to selling something – like new or used cars, car parts or insurance. But regardless of whether you're in the market for buying anything at the moment, many of them are still well worth checking out for the general tips and advice they offer. Here are a few to get you started – but do a bit of surfing around and you'll probably discover your own favourites:

- ⌖ www.honestjohn.co.uk – new and used car reviews – covering all popular models since 1990. The site includes an impressive FAQs section which gives detailed advice on a wide range of motoring issues. It's also possible to email Honest John himself with questions.
- ⌖ www.cars.uk.msn.com – new car reviews and features on all aspects of motoring.
- ⌖ www.whatcar.com – the site linked to *What Car?* magazine – readable features and car reviews. If you're interested in buying a car then try out the search feature whereby you enter a potential make together with your budget and postcode and are shown a range of possible cars near you.
- ⌖ www.evecars.com – Evecars is the female face of the *What Car?* website and runs features which are particularly useful for women. They've also got a best buys section, featuring their recommended best buys in categories such as 'Cheap city car', 'Cool convertible' or 'Big family car'. If you know you want your car for a certain type of driving, such as commuting or school runs, but don't have a clue about the virtues of particular makes and models, this is a great place to come to start drawing up a shortlist.

Motoring forums

Some motoring sites have forums where users can ask and answer questions and have discussions – Honest John's 'backroom' section is a good one.

There are also forums on more general sites such as:

- ⌖ www.thestudentroom.co.uk – you're meant to be a student to join but they don't check up on you or anything. The motoring forum is active and packed with well-informed and friendly petrolheads who will answer your motoring queries.

🚗 www.handbag.com – Handbag is a very girlie site, full of celebrity gossip and fashion tips. It also has a thriving discussion board, with forums covering relationships, health, music and so on. The moderators and contributors in the motoring section are almost all female and can provide excellent advice.

Owners' clubs

There are also internet forums linked to specific models of car, run by enthusiastic owners who will be happy to offer online advice. Many also hold social events, where you can compare notes on your cars. Some are free, others have a small charge for membership. A quick internet search will lead you to one or more sites for your particular car, and you can choose whichever most takes your fancy. Here are a few examples:

🚗 www.ffoc.co.uk – the UK's official club for Ford Focus owners.

🚗 www.miniownersclub.co.uk – the National Mini Owners' Club.

🚗 www.abvwc.org.uk – the Association of British VW Clubs.

Family, friends, colleagues, mates, taxi drivers and blokes down the pub

And then of course, there's that most invaluable source of information – everyone around you.

People who know about cars generally enjoy giving advice,

so whether you're planning on buying a car, are looking for a good garage or are worried that you're not providing the necessary care and attention to keep your car thriving, then you'll find plenty of folk around willing to put in their half-penn'orth.

Taxi drivers tend to be particularly useful as they drive for a living and will probably know via their work grapevine which local garages are good and which should be avoided. If you take cabs regularly then ask several drivers and if the same garage name keeps cropping up then you know you're potentially onto something good (I say 'potentially' because of course some garages might deal fairly with experienced drivers and amateur mechanics but be unscrupulous when it comes to anyone they see as a soft touch).

Your friendly motor mechanic

If your car is being serviced and repaired at a main dealership it's unlikely that you'll ever meet the mechanic who works on your car – the protocol there involves corralling you in a plush waiting area, as far away from anything to do with grease and sprockets as possible and plying you with free filter coffee in an effort to distract you from how frighteningly expensive they are.

If you're going to an independent garage, then there's a reasonable chance you can meet the guy who will actually work on your car, discuss any problems and talk about how you can keep your car happy and healthy in the future. If your only experience of mechanics so far has involved some oily bloke patronizing you while also staring at your breasts and ripping you off for large wodges of cash, you may feel this scenario is rather unlikely. But don't be disheartened.

There are some fantastic motor mechanics out there –

skilled, honest and happy to explain things. Chapter 4, 'Keep Your Motor Running', will help you track one down and when you have, value him or her as much as you do your favourite hairstylist, if not more.

Get a range of opinions

But even as you're gleaning all this advice it's important to remember that, with the best will in the world, some people might be giving you information that's out of date. Cars have changed dramatically over the past twenty years – they might look pretty much the same on the outside, but the internal workings are far more complex and difficult to get at. Rather than someone opening the bonnet, fiddling about a bit, shaking their head and drawing air in through their teeth to indicate a problem, this is now done by specialist computers which garages plug into your car to perform 'diagnostics' (diagnosing what the fault is). Combine this with the fact that much of the engine of modern cars is now covered over and inaccessible to the amateur mechanic, and you're looking at a situation where taking mechanical advice from someone who hasn't done hands-on work on a car for a while is a bit like learning about secretarial work from someone who retired when they were still using typewriters and taking carbon copies of everything.

This is one of the reasons why it's a good idea to get a range of opinions when it comes to anything to do with your car. Another is that you'll realize that even among people who are knowledgeable about motoring matters there can be significant differences of opinion and that The Truth about the Best Way to Buy and Run a Car isn't something that's been carved in tablets of stone, carried down a mountain and then only revealed to a privileged few. It's something that anyone can learn the basics of, and then it's just a matter of making your own mind up.

> *I was interested in buying a Fiat Panda and emailed my friends and family to ask what they think – one cousin who's really into cars raved about his and said they were fun, stylish and economical and that I should get one. But then a mate of mine who's a keen amateur mechanic said I shouldn't touch one with a bargepole and that Fiat stands for Fix It Again Tomorrow. I respect both their opinions so it was difficult to know whose advice to follow. But overall the Fiat got more thumbs-downs than ups so in the end I got a Ford Ka instead.* Salma, 27

Motoring paperwork made easy

Everything these days seems to come with mountains of paperwork attached and sadly your car is no exception.

If you're new to owning a car it can all seem quite complicated – and matters aren't improved by the fact that some of the key items are commonly referred to by more than one name (for example, Vehicle Excise Duty is also called Road Tax and the V5 Certificate is often referred to as the logbook).

However, it's not so bad once you get used to it and keeping your motoring paperwork up to date and in one place will make life a lot easier. It'll help you plan ahead for important events like your car's annual MOT test or renewing insurance and will be vital if you come to sell it. It's a legal requirement to take some of these documents when you're driving overseas. Also, a lot of this paperwork is interdependent – for example, when you tax your car at the post office you'll need your insurance and MOT certificate, or if you need to make an insurance claim the firm might want the date of your last MOT and so on.

The following five items are legal requirements – so make sure you've got them and keep them updated. Apart from the road-tax disc, which needs to be displayed on the car windscreen, it's important *not* to keep these documents in the car – nothing would make life easier for a thief hoping to sell your car than to have them all conveniently to hand! Also, if your car was involved in an accident or fire then they might be destroyed and that would make matters even more of an administrative nightmare than they would be anyway.

There's lots of useful information online about the various legal and paperwork issues related to your car and it goes into more detail than is possible here. Your best starting point is www.direct.gov.uk/motoring, where you can then follow the links to download various forms, find the address of your local DVLA (Driver and Vehicle Licensing Agency) office and so on.

1. Vehicle Registration Document

This is also called the V5 or V5/C (the latter being the more up-to-date European standard version brought out from January 2004). And sometimes it is called the logbook, which can be confusing as it's not a book at all, more a sort of leaflet.

Don't even think of buying a car that doesn't have a Vehicle Registration Document (or trust a seller who says they don't have it to hand but they'll put it in the post) – it's a red flag saying you're looking at a stolen car.

The registration document is the car's 'birth certificate' and shows the date it was first registered, engine size, body type, colour, number of previous keepers, etc. It also gives the Vehicle Identification Number (VIN) which is stamped on the car, usually somewhere in the engine bay. At the top of the document is the name of the 'registered keeper'. The keeper isn't necessarily the legal owner but the person who has charge of the car – that is, drives it and takes care of it on a day-to-day basis. Usually they're one and the same, but there are exceptions, such as parents buying a car for their child but retaining legal ownership of it.

When you buy a car you need to let the DVLA know that you're now the registered keeper as soon as possible. In the case of a brand-new car then the dealer will usually arrange for the vehicle to be registered for you. If you're buying a second-hand vehicle the current registration document will include sections that must be filled in by both the buyer and seller and posted off to the DVLA. It's important that both of you get this right and that nothing gets mislaid, forgotten about or lost in the post. You get a small section – the 'new keeper supplement' – to tide you over until the full registration document with your name at the top arrives. This should happen after four to six weeks. If it doesn't, then contact the DVLA and get it sorted out.

If you make any major changes to the car (such as altering the colour) then you need to inform the DVLA of this by filling in the relevant bit of the registration document and sending it off to them. You're also legally required to keep them up to date with any changes of address. If you lose the document you'll have to complete a V62 (application form for a registration certificate) available from the post office or by downloading the form from www.direct.gov.uk/motoring.

If you go on to sell your car it's vital to do the paperwork for transferring it to the new keeper – otherwise if your car goes on to acquire speeding or parking tickets in its new life, they'll be sent to you! See it as making sure you have a 'clean-break divorce'.

And if your car becomes so dilapidated that it needs to be scrapped then you'll need to take it to an Authorised Treatment Facility (yes, even scrapyards have ridiculously fancy titles these days). They will then take your registration document and issue you with a Certificate of Destruction (which is like a death certificate, only for a car). It's a good idea to hang on to this for several years, in case some mad computer glitch occurs and you're bombarded with demands for, say, road tax for your non-existent vehicle.

2. MOT Certificate

You only need one of these if your car is over three years old. A valid MOT (Ministry of Transport) Certificate is issued following a successful MOT test and lasts for one year. The test involves a number of checks to ensure the vehicle meets basic minimum standards of roadworthiness and 'getting the car through its MOT test' can be the source of nail-biting anxiety for many owners of older vehicles. With only a couple of exceptions, it's illegal to drive a car without a valid MOT certificate – see Chapter 4, 'Keep Your Motor Running', for more details about the test.

Among other things, the car's mileage on the testing date is noted so it's important to keep all the old MOT certificates so that when you come to sell the car it will help prove the mileage shown on the clock is genuine.

All MOT testing stations have now been connected to a central database where all the test results are held online. If you lose your MOT certificate you can get a duplicate from any MOT testing station.

3. Road Tax (also known as Vehicle Excise Duty or VED)

All cars registered in the UK must display a road-tax disc (the official term is the Vehicle Excise Licence) on the bottom left-hand side of the windscreen.

For cars registered before 1 March 2001 the rate of this tax depends on the engine size. For cars first registered on or after 1 March 2001 the rate depends on the level of carbon dioxide (CO_2 emissions). From 2009 there will be thirteen car tax bands, with the least emitting vehicles paying no road tax at all, and the 'gas guzzlers' paying up to £405. Full details about the VED rates, how they relate to emissions and which cars fit into which band can be found at www.vcacarfueldata.org.uk.

You can renew your road tax from the fifteenth day of the month in which your current disc expires. It can be renewed at most larger post offices – you'll need to take the reminder you'll have been sent by the DVLA along with your insurance certificate and the car's MOT certificate.

Alternatively you can do it online at www.direct.gov.uk/taxdisc or over the phone on 0870 850 4444 and they'll send you your disc through the post about four days later. In this instance you don't need to have the above documents to hand as your insurance and MOT details are checked electronically. You can buy a disc to last for twelve or six months, though it is cheaper to opt for the former. If for any reason you decide to take your car off the road you can get a refund for the 'unused' months.

It's important to pay your road tax on time as all the details are held on a computer and if you're overdue then you're automatically issued with an £80 fine and if you really dawdle over it you can end up having your car seized and crushed!

Cars exempt from road tax

Some cars are exempt from road tax, though they still need to display a road-tax disc. A 'free' tax disc is issued which needs to be renewed each year. These include cars used by disabled people who are eligible for certain benefits, and cars built before 1 January 1973, which are designated as 'historic vehicles'.

Becoming exempt from road tax by declaring your car 'off-road'

If your car won't be driven for some time (for example if it's undergoing major repairs or you'll be working abroad) you can 'declare your vehicle off-road' and don't need to pay road tax during this period. However, off-road does mean just that. Not driving the car isn't enough to be exempt – you're not allowed to have it parked on the street during this time but have to keep it in a garage or on a private drive.

To do this you'll need to make a SORN (Statutory Off-Road Notification) declaration, which you can do at the post office or at the same web address and phone number as for taxing the car.

4. Car insurance documents

Car insurance is quite a complicated subject and has been given a chapter all to itself – Chapter 9, 'Car Insurance Uncovered'. Keep all the documents related to your car insurance safe and easily to hand. If you renew your road tax at the post office then you'll need to show them your Certificate of Insurance – and you'll also need to show all your documents to the police if you're involved in an accident.

5. Your driving licence

Your driving licence comes in two parts – the credit-card-sized photocard licence and a paper counterpart. The photocard licence has to be updated every ten years in order to keep up with any drastic makeovers or the general ravages of time on your appearance.

The paper counterpart has more detailed information such as any driving convictions and this is what you send off to the DVLA to inform them of any change of address. If you don't, then you could end up with a large fine.

You need to be able to produce both the photocard and paper counterpart if requested by the police. Employers who need you to drive for work and some car hire companies will want to see both parts.

Your UK driving licence allows you to drive in any European Community/European Economic Area (EC/EEA) country and you must take it with you when you drive abroad in these countries. However, you're also bound by the age restrictions in these countries (some of which have 18 as the legal age for driving) so check these out before you set off. If you want to venture further afield you may need to get an International Driving Permit (IDP).

Your driving licence will be valid until you're 70, but after that date you're required to renew it and fill in a form confirming that you're still fit to drive. If your driving licence is lost or stolen then inform both the police and the DVLA as soon as possible. And if, once you've been given a replacement, you find the original one, you've got to let the DVLA know as it's an offence to hold two licences.

Incidentally, holding a car licence also qualifies you to drive a tractor or road roller – and you never know when that might come in useful!

The zen of car paperwork

So OK, you've got all the documents you need to stay legal, together with a whole load of other car-related bumph. But where are you going to put them? For most of us the temptation is to shove them into a drawer together with all the other boring, incomprehensible stuff like pension policies.

But there is another, better way – creating a car file! Keeping those essential bits of paper in a nice file makes them more approachable somehow. And it also provides a useful place to put other motoring-related bumph such as child-seat instructions.

The ideal scenario is to have both a file and a folder or box file (and if you're the sort of girl who loves any excuse to go mad in Paperchase, then you'll already be finding this idea appealing). Go for an attractive matching set if you can – or you might want to brighten up a plain file by putting a picture of your car on the front!

In your car file you can have clear A4 pockets to put various bits of paperwork related to your car such as:

- Vehicle registration document
- Current and past MOT certificates
- The service book for your car, or records of past services – these are covered in more detail in Chapter 4, 'Keep Your Motor Running' – but the more detailed the service records you've got for your car the more proof you've got that it's been properly looked after. This will count in your favour when you come to sell it. It will also keep you up to date about when different maintenance tasks were carried out and will enable you to work out when they'll need to be done again. This will put you on the right track for being able to make knowledgeable remarks such as, 'it's

been almost 40,000 miles since the cam-belt was last changed, so I think it's due for a new one.'

- ⊕ Receipt for your road tax
- ⊕ The paper counterpart for your driving licence
- ⊕ Other useful bits and pieces such as details of garages, pages torn from magazines or newspapers of cars you might be interested in in the future, and cuttings about good places to eat or visit off the motorway.

Car folder or box file

Some useful items might be too bulky for your file, so keep them in your car folder. These include:

- ⊕ Warranty details – if you've bought a new or used car from a dealer it will usually offer a warranty for a fixed period. Obviously you're going to hang on to it for this time period, but it's also worth keeping it for longer. Warranties can vary considerably in the sort of cover they offer and when, in the future, you buy another car, comparing your previous warranty with the one you're being offered could prove useful.
- ⊕ Car insurance paperwork – this is worth keeping over a period of several years, so you can keep an eye on what effect changes such as a house move or building up your no-claims bonus can have on your premium.
- ⊕ Breakdown cover paperwork
- ⊕ You might want to keep your child seat instructions or sat nav instructions in your folder too. Alternatively keep them in your car if you feel there might be times when family and friends will be driving your child and need to know how the seat works, or if you might be transferring the seat from one car to another (maybe on a group family holiday) and need a quick refresher on how to fit it.

Useful books to keep in your car

Your driver's manual

This is a booklet about your particular make and model of car, which gives specific information about how it works and how best to take care of it. You should be given a copy by the seller when you take delivery of the car – if you aren't, it's important to chase them for it. If there's a problem with getting it from them then it should be possible to buy a copy from the manufacturer. It's full of useful information about what all the different dials and switches on your dashboard relate to and how to operate them, the layout under your bonnet and so on. It's a good idea to keep it in your glove compartment so you can easily refer to it – if you're loading up your car at the DIY store and realize you need to put the back seats down, your manual won't be much use to you if it's sitting in a drawer at home.

If you do need to order a copy don't confuse the driver's manual with the car workshop manual, which takes a different approach. The workshop manual is designed for people who want to do their own repairs. So if you can see yourself tootling round your garage at the weekend replacing brake pads then you'll need one of these, but not otherwise.

Your in-car notebook

Keeping a car notebook (ideally one with a pen attached) in the glove compartment of your car is a really good idea, for all sorts of reasons.

If you have to stop and ask for directions, you can make a note of them on your pad.

If your car starts playing up (such as making strange tapping noises or producing unpleasant smells) you can jot down a description of what it does and under what circumstances, which will provide a useful memory-jogger when you come to describe the problem to your mechanic.

If you're involved in an accident you'll be able to make notes about what happened, write down your and the other person's details, etc. Some insurance companies provide 'accident checklist forms' with all the information you'll need to gather at the scene laid out and if yours does this then it's a good idea to keep a copy in the glove compartment.

And it's a useful tool for helping you stay on top of your finances. Making a note when you pay out for fuel, parking or a trip through the car wash means that you can assess these costs on a monthly or yearly basis, together with other outgoings such as insurance and road tax, and work out how much your car is really costing you to run. This is covered in more detail in the following chapter, 'Money and Your Motor', which will help you run your car without having to sacrifice too many holidays or handbags!

Chapter 2

Money and Your Motor

Some people are very switched on about their finances – they keep records and spreadsheets and monitor best-buy websites and know off the top of their heads every detail about their money, from the interest rate on their current account to how much they spent on margarine in 2004.

If you're one of these people then you'll already be monitoring how much your car is costing you. If on the other hand you're more the sort of person who doesn't have a clue about how much their credit card bill will be until it plops onto the doormat then the chances are your idea of how much of your income your car is gobbling up is going to be pretty hazy.

But knowing how much you spend on your car, and exactly where the money goes, is great for helping you make financial decisions with clarity. For example, if you're feeling flush and in a position to splash out on a new sports car, that's great – but are you able to make the ongoing financial commitment to the higher insurance and fuel costs? Or if you've been spending a lot on repairs recently for your much-loved old car, is it time to cut your losses and buy a newer one, or should you hang on in there? Then again, maybe finding a cheaper garage or learning to do some of your own basic repairs and maintenance is the answer.

If you're keen to lighten your carbon footprint and in the market for a new car is it worth considering one of the 'greener' cars such as a Toyota Prius? Or would the higher purchase price make it uneconomical for you, despite the greater fuel efficiency?

And if you're ever in a situation where you really have to tighten your belt, knowing how much it costs to keep your car on the road will help you decide whether it's something you can cut back on and replace with other forms of transport such as bikes and buses – and how much you're likely to save if you do.

It is important to bear in mind that the cost of car ownership can be unpredictable – and often, it seems, ridiculously unfair. Although, broadly speaking, new and newish cars are more reliable than old bangers, it can be frustrating when you've paid out a sizeable chunk of your savings on a new or newish car which then keeps collapsing and demanding replacement camshafts and alternators within months of the warranty expiring, while a friend of yours who drives an old banger which appears to be held together by string and mud never has any problems and sails through every MOT with only the occasional replacement tyre required.

But such is life. If you make sensible, well-informed decisions about your car, they will pay off most of the time but not always. That's why it's important to have a 'car fund' stashed away if at all possible – some cash for repairs or to use as a down payment for a new motor.

Fuel for thought

Fuel is expensive, and getting more so.

And as with so many aspects of motoring, lots of the old rules about the best-value options are shifting. For example, diesel cars used to be seen as a more economical choice than petrol if you did a high mileage. But diesel prices have risen sharply in recent years and the potential saving has declined accordingly.

And to make matters even more bewildering, there are lots of new 'greener' fuel options on offer – biodiesel, bioethanol, LPG (liquefied petroleum gas) and electric cars. The Government

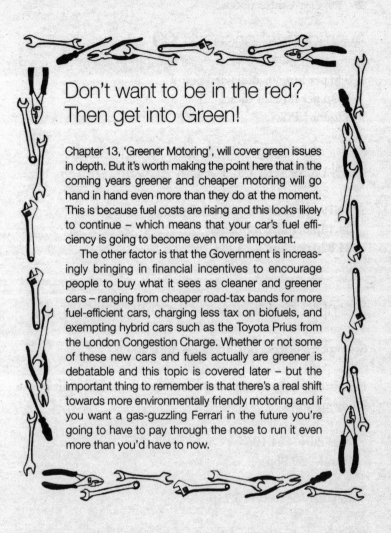

Don't want to be in the red?
Then get into Green!

Chapter 13, 'Greener Motoring', will cover green issues in depth. But it's worth making the point here that in the coming years greener and cheaper motoring will go hand in hand even more than they do at the moment. This is because fuel costs are rising and this looks likely to continue – which means that your car's fuel efficiency is going to become even more important.

The other factor is that the Government is increasingly bringing in financial incentives to encourage people to buy what it sees as cleaner and greener cars – ranging from cheaper road-tax bands for more fuel-efficient cars, charging less tax on biofuels, and exempting hybrid cars such as the Toyota Prius from the London Congestion Charge. Whether or not some of these new cars and fuels actually are greener is debatable and this topic is covered later – but the important thing to remember is that there's a real shift towards more environmentally friendly motoring and if you want a gas-guzzling Ferrari in the future you're going to have to pay through the nose to run it even more than you'd have to now.

has been imposing less tax on these fuels as a way of keeping their costs down and encouraging people to use them.

When assessing the cost of the different fuels and working out which would be best for you, it's important to be aware of the fact that the price is influenced by two main factors – the cost of the fuel itself, and then the cost of the tax on it.

Average fuel prices 2009

93p per litre for unleaded petrol
103p per litre for diesel
52p for LPG

Fuel duty (as of 1 April 2009)

54.19p per litre for unleaded petrol
54.19p per litre for diesel
24.82p per litre for LPG

Sample breakdown of costs for petrol

(www.petrolprices.com, accessed April 2009)

If a litre of unleaded petrol cost 93p it would be split in the following ways:

Fuel duty – 54.19p
Petrol – 30.98p
VAT – 12.13p
Retailer/delivery – 5.71p

If a litre of diesel costs 103p the split goes like this:

Fuel duty – 54.19p
Diesel – 27.82p
VAT – 13.43p
Retailer/delivery – 7.57p

As you can see, a large percentage of what you pay for petrol and diesel goes towards fuel duty rather than on the product itself, or to the retailer. This is a fact that many motorists get agitated about, as they feel it makes driving prohibitively expensive. However, it's currently a fact of life and one you need to be aware of when deciding what fuel to run your vehicle on. But it's not a good idea to make impulsive decisions and, for example, get your car adapted for LPG without thinking through the possible long-term financial consequences. Many people who invested in more expensive diesel cars because of their greater fuel economy are now, in the face of rising diesel prices, wondering if it was such a great decision. That's not to say that it isn't a good idea to change to the cheapest fuel source you can – just that it's a decision that has to be researched thoroughly and with reference to your particular circumstances.

How much do you spend on fuel?

Working out the exact fuel costs for your car is really useful, as it'll help you see how much you spend on fuel every month, how important fuel economy is for any new vehicle you might buy and also the cost of individual journeys – then you can decide whether it's more thrifty to do them in your car or to use public transport.

> *My nearest city is 15 miles away. If I'm going in for a Saturday shopping trip and take the bus it's £5 return. If I drive it's 16p a mile (£4.80) for petrol, with parking about £5 on top of that – a total of £9.80. I prefer driving, but I'm on a tight budget at the moment so unless I'm buying something heavy or difficult to carry I'll take public transport.* Adele, 17

Working out how many miles per gallon your car does

Let your fuel gauge drop down low.

Fill up your tank to the brim (and make a note of the cost of the fuel).

Press the trip meter on your dashboard to set it to zero (this is different from the odometer which records the overall mileage of your car).

Drive around until the fuel gauge has dropped down low again.

Check how many miles you've done.

Then it's (x miles) divided by fuel used (y gallons) = (z miles per gallon)

To convert litres to gallons, divide litres by 4.546

Example – Adele's car's m.p.g.

Adele has a Vauxhall Astra which does 240 miles on 34 litres of petrol.

34 divided by 4.546 = 7.47 gallons
240 miles divided by 7.47 gallons = 32 miles per gallon

Be aware that your car won't necessarily match the advertised fuel consumption. A study by *What Car?* magazine showed that on average a car's economy falls 6 m.p.g. below the manufacturer's claim – it's quite usual to expect an average of 42 m.p.g. and end up with an average of 35 m.p.g. Town driving, where you're always stopping and starting, uses up more fuel per mile than motorway cruising, so that's also something to bear in mind.

Working out how much you pay per mile for fuel

The amount of fuel needed to fill up your tank (litres) x (cost per litre) = cost of full tank.

Work out how many miles you can travel on a full tank.

Then the formula is (the cost of filling up) divided by (the number of miles).

Example – Adele's fuel costs per mile

Adele buys her petrol at 93p per litre and it takes 34 litres to fill her tank = £31.62 to fill up.

On a full tank (£31.62), Adele covers 240 miles.

£31.62 divided by 240 = 13p

Adele pays 13p a mile for fuel.

Tips for keeping your fuel costs down

Buy the best-value fuel you can

Check out www.petrolprices.com – this site monitors forecourt fuel prices around the UK and is simple to use: just enter your postcode or town and the system lists the nearest filling stations within ten miles, together with their current prices.

In April 2009 within a particular postcode the average price of unleaded petrol within a ten-mile radius was 95p. The highest was 98.9p, the cheapest 92.9p. Although these are just pennies, if you do a high mileage the savings over a year can run into hundreds of pounds.

Motorway service stations have a reputation for charging

higher prices – sometimes as high as an extra five to six pence per litre, so avoid paying over the odds by filling up locally whenever possible.

Drive in a fuel-efficient way

You can make your fuel go further by adopting an 'eco-driving' style which involves strategies such as avoiding rapid accelerating and braking, keeping tyres properly inflated and avoiding carrying excess baggage. This is covered in full detail in Chapter 13, 'Greener Motoring'. If you do 15,000 miles a year, then improving your driving style has the potential to save you about £200. This more relaxed way of driving will also be kinder on your engine, meaning that it is less likely to break down.

Share the cost of your fuel with someone else

Whether that's driving into work with a colleague or taking fewer cars when you go on a group holiday, splitting fuel costs can help keep costs down. And as many cities are now introducing car-sharing lanes, you'll also have a quicker and cheaper journey into town.

If you're buying a new car then make fuel economy a priority

When you're deciding between different models, check out how much it's likely to cost you for fuel. A really useful website is www.vcacarfueldata.org.uk – it lets you both look up the average m.p.g. (in both urban and extra-urban (out of town) situations) and see how much you'd pay for enough fuel to cover 12,000 miles.

Cars that are currently shining in the fuel-economy stakes include:

Petrol
Toyota Yaris – 52 m.p.g.
Toyota Aygo – 61.4 m.p.g.

Petrol/electric hybrid
Honda Civic Hybrid saloon – 61.4 m.p.g.
Toyota Prius – 65 m.p.g.

Diesel
Citroën C1 – 61.4 m.p.g.
VW Polo 3 – 74.3 m.p.g.

A quick update on diesel

Diesel cars have tended to be seen as a cheaper option for drivers doing high mileages or using large cars such as 4x4s as they tend to be more fuel-efficient. To give you an idea of the scale, an AA report stated that the average fuel efficiency of eight best-selling UK diesels was 53.95 m.p.g. as opposed to 39.95 for the equivalent petrol cars. The initial outlay would be greater, as diesels cost on average about £1400 more than their petrol equivalent, but the idea was that you'd get that cost back over time.

However, recently the cost of diesel has risen above petrol – this means that it takes longer for drivers to recoup the extra cost of a diesel car. Rising fuel prices – and the fact that if diesel prices continue to rise you'll get a lower price for your diesel car when you come to sell it – means that it's important to stay up to date with any changes to the situation and think carefully when it comes to making any decisions about buying a new car.

It's all about you

But of course, fuel is only one of the costs involved in keeping your motor running. There are lots of other variables including the cost of the car itself, insurance, road tax and repairs, to name only a few. There are also those extra costs that can easily slip under the radar, from car-wash charges to parking tickets.

When it comes to assessing how much your car is costing you and where you could economize, you need first to have a clear idea of exactly where your money is going and be honest about where you ought to cut down. After all, there's not a lot of point in always being conscientious about filling up at the petrol station where fuel is 2p a litre cheaper if you then go on to rack up lots of parking fines! An excellent website for advice on every aspect of saving money on your motoring costs is www.moneysavingexpert.com, run by financial journalist Martin Lewis.

The costs involved in running a car and how to keep them down

Let's say you need a new skirt and you see one for £40 and another for £70. If you go for the cheaper option you've saved £30. Unfortunately it is nowhere near as simple as that with cars! The different issues you need to consider when buying a car are covered in detail in Chapters 7 and 8, 'Getting Beyond "I'd Like a Pink One"' and 'Gotta New Motor?' But to touch briefly on them here, these are some of the issues you'll need to be aware of when buying a car:

The cost of the car itself

Clearly a £4000 car will be initially cheaper than a £7000 one. But if the £4000 one then needs loads of repairs, has poor fuel economy or is expensive to insure, then all of a sudden it doesn't look like such a bargain. But then again, as mentioned previously, some cheap cars can also be trouble-free and inexpensive to run. Each case has to be decided on its individual merits. Thorough research is the key – though as many mechanics will admit, a good dollop of luck helps too!

The cost of car finance

If you need to take out a loan for your car, this is the extra cost of the interest you'll be paying on top of the initial purchase price.

Depreciation

This is the loss of value of your car over time – and is some-thing most people only notice when they come to sell their cars and realize how much less they're likely to get for it than they originally paid. Some cars lose their value more quickly than others, and new cars lose their value most rapidly. It's also affected by mileage and the general condition of the car. This means that when buying a car that you plan to sell later you choose a model which is likely to hold its value. But if you're planning on staying together for years and years then it's less of a big deal.

Road tax

This was covered in the 'Motoring paperwork made easy' section in Chapter 1. If you've already got a car then the road tax for it is fixed, but when you next buy one do research the road tax for that particular model beforehand on www.vcacarfueldata.org.uk.

Insurance

This is a complex topic and as such gets a chapter all of its own – Chapter 9, 'Car Insurance Uncovered'. If you're a young or relatively new driver, drive a high-performance car or have points on your licence then your insurance is likely to be quite high. This means that the difference between quotes is likely to be substantial too – maybe hundreds of pounds. However, if you're a long-term driver with a good record then your insurance will be fairly modest and any savings will be proportionally smaller.

> *My insurance premium is £225 but I kept hearing how important it was to get the best deal so I spent an afternoon on the internet putting my details in and shopping around. But the best offer I got was £205 and, frankly, I didn't consider the £20 saving worth giving up that much of my precious free time for.* Lydia, 44

Repairs and MOT costs

The best way to keep your repair costs down is to cherish and nurture your car! Look after it as you would a much-loved pet. Perform the regular checks outlined in Chapter 4, 'Keep Your Motor Running', get it serviced at the intervals advised in your car handbook and if it starts behaving in a way that indicates it's out of sorts – weird sounds, smells or handling problems – then get it to a garage sooner rather than later and nip any potential problems in the bud.

There are few things more annoying than having to pay out wodges of cash to have your car repaired when you know it could easily have been prevented. Even worse, you could damage your car irredeemably and have to pay out for a new one.

It's also important to find a garage that you can go to for repairs, servicing and MOTs that won't rip you off – this is covered in Chapter 5. Some people aim to sidestep the whole repairs, servicing and MOT issue by buying new or newish cars which don't yet need MOTs and have long-term warranties that will cover the other charges. But of course this is more expensive in the first place. It's one of those tricky decisions that many motorists find themselves having to make and the pros and cons are discussed in Chapters 7 and 8.

Breakdown service costs

This isn't an area to economize on – there are some good-value breakdown service deals out there and it's worth having one for peace of mind. They're covered in detail in Chapter 10, 'Driving Disasters'.

Parking costs

Keep a record of parking charges in your notebook – you can keep the tickets, but they tend to fade and if you're using one of the car parks where you pay over the phone using a credit or debit card then you don't actually get a ticket – the attendant will just have your details on record.

Different car parks within the same city centre can vary in their charges, so investigate all the suitable ones to find out which is the cheapest. Consider using your local park-and-ride scheme as the cost of the bus ride into the city centre is probably going to be a lot less than a day's parking – and you'll be able to spend the final part of your journey reading or relaxing rather than inching through rush-hour congestion. It's also worth looking into renting out a parking space on someone's drive – you can arrange this via www.parkatmyhouse.com. It's free to register and if you find a suitable space you and the owner negotiate the price between yourselves.

Airport parking is notoriously expensive but the website www.airport-parking-shop.co.uk can help you get the best deal.

Congestion charge fees

At April 2009 the cost of the London Congestion Charge is £8 if you pay on or before the day of travel and £10 if you pay the following day, so paying in advance will save you money – and there are also discounts available if you drive into central London frequently. See www.tfl.gov.uk for more details.

Speeding and parking fines

The best way to avoid these charges is to stick to the speed limit and check the regulations carefully before parking anywhere! It's worth remembering that if you commit a speeding offence you've got to inform your insurers and they may well put your premium up – yet another reason to stay on the right side of the law.

Miscellaneous

This covers stuff you buy for your car – whether that's fairly cheap stuff like de-icer spray and steering wheel covers or more expensive items such as child car seats or a sat nav system. Also costs for cleaning your car, such as car washes or valets.

The prospect of trawling around to get a good deal in all these different areas can seem boring and time-consuming. But if you've got access to the internet you'll find it much easier than you might imagine – the websites listed in this chapter and in the sections on topics such as car insurance or breakdown cover can really help speed up your quest for the best bargains.

If you can, it's a good idea to channel your savings into your 'car fund' so that you'll be able to shell out for repairs at short notice if necessary. And, of course, when you next need to buy a car, the more you've got stashed away the better placed you'll be to buy the car you'd really like, as opposed to getting what-ever you can afford off Dodgy Al's Used Cars forecourt!

Chapter 3

How Clean Is Your Car?

Is your car gleaming and well cared for? Or does it look like a cross between a teenager's bedroom and a shanty town on wheels?

> *I got a new car a few months ago and it's already full of letters from school, sweet wrappers, old apple cores, empty water bottles rattling round under the passenger seat and crumbs.* Clare, 32

> *My car is filthy inside and out. Inside because I have a long-haired dog who goes everywhere with me and leaves quite a lot of him behind every time he does. Outside because I live in the middle of the countryside and whenever it rains it gets covered in mud. I do attempt to wash it every so often but honestly, what's the point?* Julia, 55

Even girls who are usually quite houseproud can easily end up with a car that's a total tip. And that's understandable, really. As you go about your daily business, it's inevitable that you're going to accumulate stuff. And then when you finally arrive home after your supermarket shop, rush-hour commute or gym visit, your main priority is going to be to get inside and fix yourself a cup of tea or a G&T rather than gather up all the accumulated junk and give everything a quick wipe down with a damp cloth.

But keeping your car clean is a really good idea, for a variety of reasons. Having dirty windows and headlights can affect visibility and make driving in poor light dangerous. A clean and well-maintained car will keep its resale value better than a tatty one. And as many of us spend a lot of time in our cars, it's going to be more agreeable if it's a place that's clean, well organized and even attractive, rather than somewhere you express your inner bag-lady. And of course, it's nice not to find yourself having to stammer embarrassed apologies every time you give someone a lift.

So here are some tips for transforming your car into a place that Kim and Aggie would be proud of:

Clean as you go

It can be quite tricky to gather up all the items which accumulate in your car when you're also trying to manhandle shopping, sports kit or children out of it as well. Make the process easier by keeping a supply of plastic carrier bags in the glove compartment (a little roll is best), chucking any rubbish into them and taking it with you every time you leave.

Another option is to invest in a Collapsible Car Bin – a container about the size of a large plant pot, which can either be hung from the car head-rest for children sitting in the back to put their old banana skins in, or hooked over the gear lever. It handily collapses down when you're not using it. They're available at Lakeland (www.lakeland.co.uk) for £3.99.

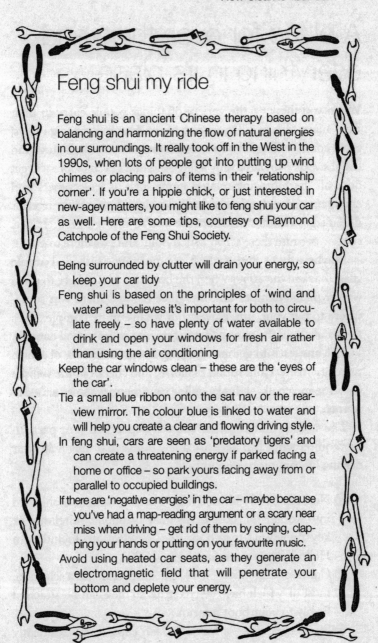

Feng shui my ride

Feng shui is an ancient Chinese therapy based on balancing and harmonizing the flow of natural energies in our surroundings. It really took off in the West in the 1990s, when lots of people got into putting up wind chimes or placing pairs of items in their 'relationship corner'. If you're a hippie chick, or just interested in new-agey matters, you might like to feng shui your car as well. Here are some tips, courtesy of Raymond Catchpole of the Feng Shui Society.

Being surrounded by clutter will drain your energy, so keep your car tidy

Feng shui is based on the principles of 'wind and water' and believes it's important for both to circulate freely – so have plenty of water available to drink and open your windows for fresh air rather than using the air conditioning

Keep the car windows clean – these are the 'eyes of the car'.

Tie a small blue ribbon onto the sat nav or the rearview mirror. The colour blue is linked to water and will help you create a clear and flowing driving style.

In feng shui, cars are seen as 'predatory tigers' and can create a threatening energy if parked facing a home or office – so park yours facing away from or parallel to occupied buildings.

If there are 'negative energies' in the car – maybe because you've had a map-reading argument or a scary near miss when driving – get rid of them by singing, clapping your hands or putting on your favourite music.

Avoid using heated car seats, as they generate an electromagnetic field that will penetrate your bottom and deplete your energy.

A place for everything and everything in its place

When you think of the variety of things people carry in their car – maps, drinks, CDs, money for parking meters, yoga mats, spare coats, wellington boots, tennis racquets, children's toys and travel sweets – to name only a few. And that's even before you get onto all the motoring-related items such as ice-scrapers and emergency triangles. It soon becomes clear that your car interior doesn't get chaotic just because you're disorganized. It gets chaotic because there's Too Much Stuff and Nowhere to Put It.

Maybe a boot and a glove compartment provided ample space back in the 1950s when the boot was somewhere to put a wicker picnic hamper and the glove compartment was somewhere to put your, um, gloves. But we live more complex lives these days, and the current arrangement just isn't good enough.

The answer is to get into cunning storage solutions, of which there are many. Hunt round Halfords, and check out the website www.me-mo.co.uk – a funky online car accessories store aimed at women.

The storage that's best for you will depend on your particular requirements. But here are a few things that may help your driving life run more smoothly.

- Non-slip car dashboard mat – turns a slippery dashboard into storage for loose items such as mobile, sunglasses or keys: www.me-mo.co.uk does a selection, including a Hello Kitty version for about £4.99.
- Car boot organizer – www.speeding.co.uk has a selection, most of which have velcro strips so they can be attached firmly to your boot interior.
- Sunglasses clip – a holder which clips sunglasses neatly

Primp my ride

While we're on the subject of the inside of your car, it's worth considering whether you might like to primp it up a bit. Many of us spend hours a day in our cars – more time than we might spend (awake) in our bedrooms. But whilst most of us will express our individual taste when decorating our bedrooms (extravagant boudoir, minimalist white space, cosy floral haven or whatever), hardly anyone gives much thought to the interior decor of their car.

'Car decoration' does, of course, have a bit of a bad rep – fluffy dice and fluffy pink seat covers spring to mind. But there are girls who like both those things and if you're one of them there's no reason not to indulge yourself – it's your car, after all!

www.me-mo.co.uk has oodles of items to make your car look more girlie – from Hawaiian-print steering wheel covers to Hello Kitty pink chrome tax disc holders and pink valve caps. And if you've always fancied one of those flower vases on the dashboards of Volkswagen Beetles, you can get one from www.roofbox.co.uk for £5.20.

onto your car's visor. You can get one for £4.99 at www.speeding.co.uk.

- ⊛ CD organizer – you can get CD organizers which clip onto your sun visor: www.speeding.co.uk do one for £5.99 with space for ten CDs and pockets for credit and business cards, receipts and spare change. If you like girlie accessories, www.me-mo.co.uk does a Tinkerbell CD organizer for £11.99.

- ⊙ In-car hanger – beloved of salesmen, an in-car hanger will allow you to arrive unrumpled by giving you somewhere to hang up coats and jackets while driving. Buy online at www.carparts-direct.co.uk, £24.99.
- ⊙ Back-seat organizers – these hang over the back of the front seat and have pockets –they're ideal for picking up the overflow of your personal possessions and for children's books and toys: www.me-mo.co.uk does a good one for £12.50.

Prevention is better than cure

When it comes to keeping your car clean, prevention is better than cure. This isn't about taking a neurotic Howard Hughes approach to cleanliness – though some girls do take having a pristine car rather seriously.

> *I'm very fussy about the inside of my car. I hate having guests in the car and make them put their feet on a newspaper instead of dirtying my car mats – it's awful but I can't help myself!* Penny, 22

Instead, it's more about thinking things through – about considering who you're going to have in your car, and what you're prepared to let them do when they're in there!

Children

If you have children, then obviously they're going to travel in the car, and you might also find yourself transporting children belonging to a friend or relative. Travelling with children is covered in detail in Chapter 12, 'Are We There Yet?'. But as far as keeping your car interior tidy goes, the main area to exercise caution in is that of drinks and snacks. 'Anything sticky or likely to drip should be a no-no,' says qualified motor mechanic and car valeter Louise A'Barrow. 'Food can get down the sides of the seats, into cracks and crevices such as around the gear lever and getting it out again can be a nightmare.'

So think ahead about which snacks will be the least messy, and choose those (apples rather than oranges, wine gums rather than chocolate). Consider having a 'water only' policy in the car for older children. Spilt orange juice is bad enough, but spilt milk is truly horrible. Allowing a child to eat an ice-cream in the car is a really, really bad idea. Even if they accuse you of being a Bad Mummy and imply that they'll need therapy later, stand firm on this one.

If your child suffers from car-sickness, then keep a supply of sick-bags in the car, and if they tell you they don't feel well then pull over as soon as possible. And of course try the strategies for preventing car-sickness later in Chapter 12.

Smokers

If you're a smoker yourself, it can be a good idea to avoid smoking in your car as the smell of smoke gets into the upholstery and can significantly lower your car's resale value. If you let your friends smoke in the car occasionally, then leaving the window open will help the smell to dissipate. But bear in mind that if they accidentally make a cigarette burn in the upholstery, it'll look horrible and be expensive to repair.

Dogs

In terms of the mess generated in your car, there's going to be a significant difference between ferrying around your Paris Hilton chihuahua or two big, hairy Golden Retrievers who like to spend their walks rolling in as many unspeakable things as possible. You can buy 'dog hammocks' to cover the back seats and footwells – or if you've got an estate car it might be a good idea to transport them in the boot.

Covering up

It's only right to end a section on preventing problems with dirt and mess by putting in a good word for car seat covers – www.me-mo.co.uk do a great range, including polka dots and flowers. Halfords do a more sober dark set for £19.99. The brilliant thing about seat covers is that they can just be whisked off and washed – much easier than trying to clean the original car upholstery. If you've got children, then consider them an essential.

Mats for the footwell of the car are also an excellent investment and will keep it looking good for much longer. Also, having removable foot mats can prove very useful for getting out of icy conditions and mud, as you can put them under the wheels to give you the grip necessary to pull away.

Your clean machine

Some drivers have the same approach to cleaning as the late Quentin Crisp, who once famously declared he never bothered because 'after the first four years, the dirt doesn't get any worse.'

Others are tremendously keen to clean, polish, wax and buff every nook and cranny, including areas such as door shuts and wheel arches which you might not even have noticed much before, let alone thought of cleaning.

It's a bit like the wide variety you find in girls' individual 'beauty regimes'. Some are perfectly happy with a quick rub over with a cleansing wipe, while others go in for lengthy sessions involving cleansing, toning, and moisturizing, combined with regular papaya face-masks and microdermabrasion.

Car cleaning is similar in that it's up to you how far you take it – but if you at least follow the guidelines below you'll have a car you can be proud of.

Cleaning the inside of your car

Vacuuming

If you're vacuuming your car at home, the best option is to use your domestic vacuum cleaner as it'll probably be far more powerful than a hand-held one – and any special upholstery attachments you've got for it will come in useful too. Either haul it out to the garage or see if you can get it to reach the car by use of extension leads.

If that's not possible, then try using a hand-held vacuum which will plug into the 12v socket in your car (what used to be called the cigarette lighter). Many garages also have car vacuums, but they can be expensive if you want to do a really thorough job and, again, tend not to be as good as domestic vacuum cleaners.

Before you get started, take out the car mats, give them a good shake and put them to one side. Then when you're vacuuming, work from the top down, doing the seats first and using the upholstery nozzle to get in between the cushions. As you're working, look out for any stains or damage to the carpet and upholstery and make a mental note to come back to it later. Finally clean the floor carpets (not forgetting under the car seats, which can get very dirty) and the boot.

Interior

The next step is to clean the dashboard and what's called the 'interior trim' (the insides of the doors, armrests, etc.). 'A damp cloth will work perfectly well for this, but if you do want to use products go for specific car-cleaning ones rather than the household variety,' says Louise A'Barrow. 'Never use any sort of polish on the steering wheel, handbrake, gear knob or pedals as that can make them slippery – just give them a wipe down. And if you're using cleaning fluid or spray always apply it to the cloth first – if you apply it directly to areas like the dashboard, it might leak through the gaps between the different components and damage the internal electric systems.'

Then clean the insides of the windows. Finally, vacuum the car mats and replace them.

What's the damage?

If your car interior does get stained or damaged, it's important to treat it as quickly as possible. It's a good idea to keep a car-upholstery cleaner in the boot, so you can pounce on any stains as soon as they appear. But if you didn't notice them at the time then tackle them as soon as you do.

Here are some tips for particular problems:

- ⊖ Chewing gum – running an ice-cube or pressing a bag of frozen peas against the gum will help harden it, making it easier to pick or scrape off.
- ⊖ Chocolate – wait until it's hardened and scrape off what you can, then use an upholstery cleaner.
- ⊖ Pet hair – a damp cloth, rubbed in one direction will bring the hairs together to form small piles which can then be picked off.
- ⊖ Spilt milk – mop up the excess with kitchen roll as soon as you can, then sprinkle the area with bicarbonate of soda, available from supermarkets in the baking aisle – you'll find it next to the baking powder. Leave it for 24 hours then vacuum and treat the area with a general upholstery cleaner. One tip for getting rid of the smell is to leave a cup of ordinary household vinegar in the car overnight. However, the effects of spilt milk are notoriously difficult to shift and you might need to take your car to a professional valeter.
- ⊖ Vomit – with car-sick children (or even tired and emotional friends) accidents do happen. But it goes without saying that this is a really nasty one to deal with! Don some rubber gloves and remove what you can, then gently dab the area using soapy warm water followed by upholstery cleaner. This is another one where you might need a valeter to really get rid of the aftermath.

Upholstery and carpets

If the car upholstery or carpets have been torn or damaged, you might be able to repair them yourself – check out Halfords for suitable products. If that's not possible then ask a valeter for advice.

Smelly car syndrome

Of course, the best way to keep a car free of nasty smells is to clean it thoroughly. But if you've bought or inherited an old banger that's had such a hard life that nothing you can do will ever make it as fresh as an alpine meadow, one trick for making it more agreeable is to put some cat litter into half a pair of tights, tie a knot in the end to seal it and put it out of sight, under the seat or in the boot. And, like the footwell mats, the cat litter can also be used around the wheels to provide grip for the tyres when it comes to getting out of muddy or icy conditions.

Other strategies include:

- ☻ Sprinkling bicarbonate of soda over the carpet and upholstery, leaving it for 24 hours then vacuuming up.
- ☻ Keeping a tumble-dryer sheet under the car seat.
- ☻ Placing a bowl of fresh coffee granules in the car overnight.
- ☻ Putting a natural sponge in the car – it'll absorb any odours.

Windows on the world

Whether you wash your car frequently or hardly at all, it's vital that you keep both the inside and outside windows sparkling at all times. When it comes to safe driving, the importance of clean windows can't be over-emphasized. Most of the time it might feel as though a bit of dirt doesn't make much difference, but when you find yourself driving at night or in strong sunshine it's another matter – grubby or even just smeary windscreens will reduce your visibility dramatically.

Don't clean your windows on a sunny day as it'll leave them with a smeary finish. You can use car window cleaning products, but many people get good results just using a damp cloth, followed by polishing the windows to a shine with a dry one. And always wipe parallel to the heated rear-window lines. If you rub vigorously in the wrong direction you risk snagging any cuts around the film and tearing them.

'If your windscreen doesn't come up sparkling after that, then it's probably because it's suffering from a build-up of oily traffic film from the road,' says Vanessa Guyll, technical specialist at the AA:

> You'll need to wash it well using a cleaning product, rinse it thoroughly then lift the wipers back and clean the screen by applying methylated spirit to pieces of kitchen towel. Work on a small area of the glass before moving to the next and use a new piece of kitchen towel for each section – otherwise the oil will spread across the glass. The wiper blades should be replaced at the same time, as they will have become contaminated by the oil. Another possible reason for a dirty windscreen is because the rubber on the windscreen wipers is starting to wear and it's time to have them replaced, so check that out as well.

Cleaning the outside of your car

Bird droppings – no, they're not lucky

In fact they're extremely bad news for your paintwork. Bird droppings contain uric acid, which eats through the lacquer and paint, leaving bleached-out marks. So whether you're the sort of person who cleans their car weekly or once a year, don't hang about when it comes to bird droppings – get rid of them as soon as possible.

The best approach is to soak a sponge in car shampoo and place it on top of the droppings – leave it there for 5–10 minutes so that it softens them up before attempting to gently wipe them away. If any hard deposits remain, repeat the process – don't scrub away at it whatever you do, or you'll be in danger of lifting off the top layer of lacquer.

How often should you wash your car?

From the point of view of caring for the bodywork and protecting it against rust and corrosion, it's a good idea to wash your car about once a week in the winter – this is because the extra salt and grit on the roads can cause damage. In the summer it becomes more of an aesthetic issue – once every couple of weeks should be sufficient to keep it looking good. Your options include taking your car to a self-service car wash, hand-washing it yourself or using a hand-wash service. Whatever approach you take, use this as an opportunity to check your car over for any signs of damage such as chips in the windscreen or rust patches. Advice on dealing with these and other problems are covered in Chapter 4, 'Keep Your Motor Running'.

Working at the car wash

There are two main types of self-service car wash, the drive-through variety and the jet-wash one. Some are paid for by putting cash in the machine, with others you have to buy a token in advance. If it's the latter it's important to find that out in advance so you don't find yourself embarrassingly tokenless at the front of the queue.

Drive-through car wash

These are very convenient as you don't even have to get out of your car. Also there can be something weirdly enjoyable about the experience of being safely locked inside your vehicle and having all those brushes coming at you, blotting out the light and temporarily immersing you in this weird, soapy under-world. On the downside, if you've got any leaks in your sunroof, this is when you find out about them.

And they have other drawbacks. Tiny particles of dirt can get stuck in the rollers and become an instant scouring pad. 'You can usually spot a car that's regularly been through a car wash from the light scratches on the paintwork,' says Vanessa Guyll of the AA. So think carefully before putting your pride and joy through those rotating brushes.

Jet car wash

Jet car washes involve more effort as you have to get out of the car and wield the various brushes and attachments yourself. They're better for your car than the drive-through variety how-ever – though it's a good idea to spray the jet over the brush attachment first to get rid of dirt from the previous users. You can then give your car the right sort of going-over for its con-dition, scrubbing it down if it's muddy or finishing off with wax if you want that extra shine. However, you'll find the water gets everywhere so it's not something to do if you're wearing your best suede heels.

Also some of them are token-operated but don't give you enough time so you're left racing round like a mad thing trying to get all the suds off before it finishes. The more sensible ones are cash-operated so you can top up when it starts beeping at you – keep some spare change in your pocket for this.

Using a commercial hand-wash service

There are commercial hand-wash services available in most cities, most carried out while you wait. Some are carried out by one person, in others four people at a time will wash your car. The quality of the service offered can vary quite a bit, so it's worth asking around for recommendations for a good local one.

Commercial hand-washes – which basically involve a sponge, a bucket and a wipe with a chamois leather – shouldn't be confused with professional valeting services which do a far more thorough – and expensive – job. For details of these see the section on car valeters below.

Hand-washing your car yourself

If you want to experience the Middle England lifestyle to the full then you'll hand-wash your car every Sunday morning. If you want to live out your boyfriend's fantasy then you'll do it wearing your bikini while he watches, nursing a cold beer.

There are other advantages to hand-washing your car – you can work on it more thoroughly than an automatic or jet car wash will allow and you'll have the chance to spot any bumps or scratches and deal with them early on. Done properly, it's quite hard work so it can double up as exercise too.

What you'll need

- ⊖ The right weather – a dull or overcast day. Avoid washing your car in direct sunlight or it'll dry to a smeary finish and cold water on hot paint can sometimes cause tiny cracks in the finish.
- ⊖ Car shampoo – you'll need to invest in some proper car shampoo – don't even think of using washing-up liquid as it's much too harsh and will strip the wax from your car.

As with haircare, there are a bewildering number of brands of car shampoo, polish and wax, each of which will have its devotees – it's a bit like how some girls are Toni and Guy fans while others will only use John Frieda products. 'Carplan and Turtle Wax are good economy products, Meguiars and Autoglym are mid-range and Zymol and Swiss Wax are high end,' explains Caron Stevens of the British Valeters Organisation. 'If you're not planning on waxing your car after shampooing, then go for a shampoo with wax included as this will help protect your paintwork.'

- A bucket – for mixing the shampoo and water – and for rinsing the car if you're not using a hosepipe. Always make the shampoo/water mix to the specifications on the bottle – if you use too much shampoo it'll take you forever to wash it off.

- A car-wash mitt or sponge – car-wash mitts are the better option as they take the dirt up into the material, while sponges hold the dirt on the surface and it can get scraped across the paintwork, so if you really care about your car go for a mitt.

- Tyre brush – this isn't an essential, but if you do use a brush on the tyres, don't then go on to use it on the bodywork as it'll have picked up abrasive particles and might damage your bodywork. You can use either a cut-down old paintbrush or buy a tyre brush from a car accessories shop.

- Hosepipe – not everyone is able to use a hosepipe to rinse down their car – either because they can't park close enough to their house for it to stretch or because a hosepipe ban is operating. There's also the green issue, as many people feel that they'll use far more water with a hosepipe than with a bucket. However, an interesting report in *Auto*

Express magazine contradicts this. Researchers washed a family saloon with a hose and a bucket, and discovered that it took 30 litres and 110 litres respectively – so the bucket wasted almost four times as much water! This is because they were able to direct the water more effectively using a hose with a nozzle that switched off the flow when not in use, whereas it was more difficult to direct where the water went when using a bucket. Try both methods and see which works best for you. If you'd like to use a hose but can't get one to stretch far enough from your tap then a hand-pumped garden sprayer from a local garden centre is a worthwhile investment.

- Chamois leather or a micro-fibre towel – a chamois leather – sometimes called a chammy or shammy – is made of leather, so if you're a committed vegetarian you might prefer to use a synthetic version, many of which are just as good and last longer. You could also use a micro-fibre towel sold in car outlets such as Halfords.

The sequence of events

1. Hose or wash any excess dirt off the car, and rinse the car all over with plain water.
2. Lather up the mitt or sponge with the soapy water and start washing the bodywork, beginning at the roof and working down.
3. Open the doors and give the door shuts a wipe down.
4. Rinse thoroughly using either the bucket or hose – try to rinse with warm water, it gives a less streaky result than cold.
5. Take the chamois leather, soak it in cold water, wring it out and then use flat against the paintwork to soak up the excess water. You could also use the micro-fibre towel for this task – either will give the car a nice shiny finish.

6. Then clean the chrome bits and headlights – a good rub with bicarbonate of soda on a damp cloth works wonders.

7. Finally do the wheels – wash the tyres with the hosepipe or water from the bucket and if you've got a tyre brush then give them a scrub with it; then wash up underneath the wheel arches. If you've got alloy wheels and want them to really gleam then use an alloy wheel cleaning fluid and brush too. Never use the same sponge or brush on the wheels and then on the bodywork, as brake dust is very abrasive and will scrape your paintwork.

You should now have a sparklingly clean car – well done!

Waxing and polishing

If you really want to cherish your motor, you might decide to go on to wax and/or polish it.

- ⊕ Waxing – this seals the paintwork, giving it a protective coating.
- ⊕ Polish – this can improve the appearance of the paint.
- ⊕ Wax/Polish – you can also get combinations of these.

There's no point in having a go at any of these unless you've got the car really clean first however – otherwise you're just sealing any dirt in.

It's a good idea to wax your car about every three to six months. Follow the directions carefully and bear in mind that it's a task that requires a fair bit of elbow grease and don't embark on it when you're in a hurry.

Polishing is a more major job, and not one to undertake

lightly as, although it's great for bringing shine to weathered or dull paint, it can be quite abrasive. It's advisable to go for wax first as it'll give a great shine but be kinder to your paintwork.

A more advanced form of polishing is to use a paint renovator, such as T-Cut. This is more abrasive than a normal polish and takes off a very thin layer of the paintwork, so that tiny scratches will be evened out – but should only be considered as a last resort. 'Be very cautious about using a paint renovator unless you're an expert,' says Caron Stevens. 'It's a hard product to use and you could end up in a worse mess than you started.'

Taking things up a notch

It's great to have a clean car – and taking things further and having a shiny, pristine one that looks as if it's just come out of the showroom can be even better. If the car-cleaning bug gets you and you want to keep your motor as well-cared-for as possible, then you'll be getting into more advanced procedures and need the products to carry them out. Get yourself down to your local car accessories shop, which will provide you with all your heart could possibly desire to keep your motor looking gorgeous – you'll find brushes for the tyres, brushes for the wheel spokes, special products for buffing up the chrome and the bumpers – the works!

Even if you're not interested in keeping your car quite that pristine normally, it can be worth pushing the boat out and making a real effort if you're planning to sell it. It's a bit like all those endless property programmes which give advice on how to smarten up your house to make it attractive to buyers – think of it as the motoring equivalent of painting everything white and filling the house with the smell of baking bread. And if you don't want to take on that job yourself, it might be worth investing in a car valeting service.

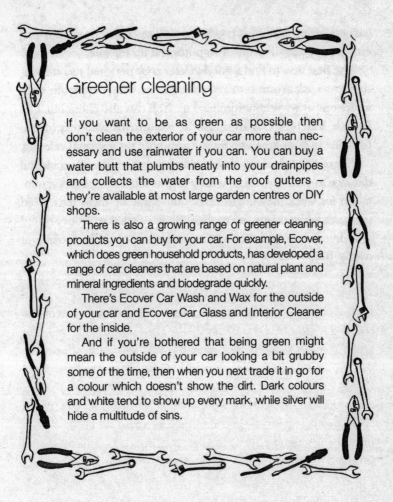

Greener cleaning

If you want to be as green as possible then don't clean the exterior of your car more than necessary and use rainwater if you can. You can buy a water butt that plumbs neatly into your drainpipes and collects the water from the roof gutters – they're available at most large garden centres or DIY shops.

There is also a growing range of greener cleaning products you can buy for your car. For example, Ecover, which does green household products, has developed a range of car cleaners that are based on natural plant and mineral ingredients and biodegrade quickly.

There's Ecover Car Wash and Wax for the outside of your car and Ecover Car Glass and Interior Cleaner for the inside.

And if you're bothered that being green might mean the outside of your car looking a bit grubby some of the time, then when you next trade it in go for a colour which doesn't show the dirt. Dark colours and white tend to show up every mark, while silver will hide a multitude of sins.

Car valeters – calling in the professionals

If you've got smells, stains or general damage to your car that you haven't been able to fix then it's time to turn to a professional valet. You can use them for a particular problem (such as spilt milk or an upholstery tear) or get a thorough valet (involving taking the seats out, steam-cleaning both them and the carpets, using specialist products, etc.) to smarten up your car, either for yourself or prior to putting it up for sale.

The best way to find a good valeter is by personal recommendation so ask around, or try asking in an internet forum such as the one at www.honestjohn.co.uk. You can also check out The British Valeters Organisation at www.britishvaleters.org to find one in your area and for advice about professional valeting.

A professional valeter should have insurance against accidental damage to your car and be willing to give you a no-obligation quotation for work they might carry out. Some of them have fixed premises while others are mobile. Basic valets start from around £30 but if you want the whole works you could be looking at over £100.

Chapter 4

Keep Your Motor Running

Cars ain't what they used to be

One of the most important things to know about cars is that they've changed hugely in the last couple of decades. We're all aware of the massive shifts in technology in other areas of our lives. Years ago computers were these big clunky machines that had to be attended to by scientists in lab coats carrying clipboards. Now they're as slim as magazine supplements and five-year-olds play games on them.

Cars, on the other hand, look pretty much the same externally as they ever did. But underneath the bonnet it's a very different matter. Twenty or even ten years ago your average amateur mechanic could open it up and get stuck in with a spanner. But now much of the car's inner workings such as brakes, bulbs and windscreen wipers are controlled by electronic systems. All these components have to communicate with each other and this happens via various computer-driven codes and software. So if there's a problem the answer is often going to involve taking the car to a garage to be hooked up to some relevant 'diagnostic equipment'. And in many cases even if you do buy and fit new parts the car won't actually work properly until the garage systems input the right computer codes to make the car recognize and accept them.

There's also a lot more packed in under the bonnet these days. 'Cars have lots of equipment they didn't used to have before, such as air conditioning and emission-control equipment,' explains Vanessa Guyll, technical expert at the AA. 'There's a lot less space for mechanics to work in and it can be frustrating if you're not experienced – or even if you are!'

These facts are really important to bear in mind when it comes to making decisions about caring for your car. They will influence the choice between going to a franchised dealership or using a local garage, whether you fit a headlamp bulb yourself and whether you allow someone else (even someone who claims to know what they're doing) to jump-start their car off your battery. All these issues will be dealt with in this and later chapters – but the main thing to bear in mind is that cars are far more advanced, more complicated and also in some respects more easy to damage than they used to be. Basically, it's all a very far cry from the days when you could repair a fan-belt using a pair of ladies' stockings.

But even though the opportunities for tinkering about under the bonnet are becoming increasingly limited, this doesn't provide a get-out clause when it comes to caring for your car. Whether you're driving a high-tech car with the latest number-plate or have an ancient VW camper van, it's still vitally important to do the weekly checks and understand the basics of driving and caring for it so you can have years of safe and carefree motoring together.

Caring for your car

Many of us take our cars for granted. We get behind the wheel and expect them to take us wherever we want to go without any problems or fuss. And most of the time, they do. But then there are occasions when they break down or cost us a fortune in repairs and it's all very traumatic. Sometimes repairs and breakdowns are unavoidable – but often they're not. They're down to neglecting the basic needs of the car for care and attention. The fact is that if you want your car to look after you, then you're going to have to look after it.

See it as something which needs to be nurtured, like a friend-ship or a pet. The tasks involved are pretty simple once you understand what needs doing and have got the hang of them. And on the plus side they're far less time-consuming than lis-tening to late-night ranty phone calls from your best mate about her boyfriend's latest transgressions and nowhere near as dis-agreeable as cleaning out the cat-litter tray.

Here's what you need to do to keep you and your car safe and reliable.

Drive carefully

Harsh braking, fast cornering, revving the engine – these boy-racer driving techniques will thrash your poor car and hasten its demise. Driving smoothly means your car will have fewer prob-lems and last longer. And if your parking can be a bit slapdash then it's worth brushing up on that as well, because scraping the kerb is really bad for your tyres.

Act promptly

If your car develops a problem, such as leaking fluids, being slow to start, making odd noises or smells, then it's really important not to ignore it. The same applies if any of the warning lights on your dashboard come on to alert you of certain faults. 'Don't expect your car to just get better by itself because it probably won't,' says Vanessa Guyll. 'And the longer you leave it the greater the chance of the damage getting worse and even more expensive to repair. Don't put your own or anyone else's safety at risk by driving it – call a garage for advice immediately.' It's also worth remembering that if a car is under warranty the manufacturer is within their rights to reject a claim if they can prove you ignored a warning light.

Service regularly

Most people know they should have their car serviced regularly, but many of us are a bit vague about what a service actually involves, other than that it's probably got something to do with having the oil changed. Services are covered in more detail in Chapter 6, but basically, they involve two main aspects – one is actually doing stuff, like changing oil or air filters, the other is checking stuff like brakes and batteries. It's a bit like when you go for a dental check-up and hygienist visit – your dentist will make sure there aren't any loose fillings or a pressing need to have your wisdom teeth out, and your hygienist will get your mouth in tip-top condition.

Do the basic car maintenance checks

If servicing is the equivalent of a dental check-up, then the car checks and maintenance are the equivalent of brushing and flossing regularly. However, some women find the prospect distinctly unappealing.

I don't know how to use one of those tyre pressure gauges and don't know what the reading should be anyway. Jennifer, 31

I don't do the checks – not really sure how. Under the bonnet is a scary place and I know I'd put oil where the screen wash is meant to go. All that stuff gives me a mental block. Laura, 24

But even if dealing with anything even vaguely mechanical currently feels out of your comfort zone, this really is non-negotiable. Tyres which aren't properly inflated could lead to a puncture when you're travelling at 70 m.p.h. down the motorway, a brake fluid leak could mean you're unable to stop when approaching a busy junction – skimping on the checks means putting your own and other people's safety at risk. Neglecting them can also lead to expensive repairs or even the complete breakdown of your car.

My first ever car was an old Ford Escort – I loved it and we went everywhere together. Then one day I was driving along when the engine overheated and I had to pull over. Checking under the bonnet I realized I'd forgotten to top up the radiator and it had run completely dry. I didn't have any water in the car so I ended up racing to a nearby shop and buying litres of still mineral water that I poured in. Somehow I got it back home, but it never recovered from the damage and it had to be scrapped. I felt really guilty – as if I'd 'killed' my car through my neglect. Also, I was skint at the time and couldn't afford to buy another one for almost a year. Clare, 32

However, the good news is that doing the checks isn't really scary at all – it's just something that feels like venturing into unknown territory for many of us. Once you've consulted your car handbook and run through the checks a few times you'll realize how easy they actually are and how quickly you can do them. Just put aside a few minutes a week, and you're sorted!

POWDER-ing your car

A useful approach to remembering the checks you need to do is to follow the **POWDER** sequence below.

> P – petrol
> O – oil
> W – windscreen washer and other fluid levels
> D – damage to the vehicle
> E – electrics (lights)
> R – rubber (tyres and windscreen wipers)

You'll need your driver's manual – this will show the geography of what goes where under the bonnet and get you past any 'oil in the brake fluid container' anxiety attacks. The checks should be done when the car is parked on level ground and the engine is cold. It's a good idea to do them at the same time every week, so you get into a routine. 'Weekly checks will help you to get a feel for your car and talk more knowledgeably to the garage if a problem does develop,' says Vanessa Guyll of the AA.

Try to avoid getting any of the fluids on your skin and have a clean cloth handy so you can wipe them off immediately if necessary. And of course wash your hands thoroughly as soon as the checks are completed. If you've got sensitive skin then it's a good idea to wear a pair of plastic disposable gloves.

Always put the caps of the various containers back on firmly. And if you lose the tyre valve caps, get some replacements as soon as you can – they're on sale at most garages. If there's a problem with any of the items such as windscreen wipers or bulbs and you want to have a go at replacing them you'll have to get the right parts – they're on sale at car parts shops like Halfords or over the internet at sites such as Car Parts Direct (www.carparts-direct.co.uk). To get the right ones you'll need to know the make, model and year of your car – and maybe even the Vehicle Identification Number. Another option is to take along the old part and get an identical one. Some of these tasks can be a bit fiddly, so if you have the chance to get an experienced friend or your local mechanic to show you how to do it the first time that's ideal.

An alternative to taking your car to a garage for the smaller jobs is to use the We-Fit service at Halfords' larger stores. Basically, the deal is that you buy the part from them and then one of their trained staff will fit it for you for a reasonable fee – sample prices are £2.99 for car bulbs, £1.99 for mirror glass and so on. They also do a free five-point Car Health Check – covering battery, wiper blades, bulbs, oil level and screen wash. Phone your local store for details and to find out if you'll need to book in advance.

P – petrol (or other fuel)

Why

The worst-case scenario is that if you don't keep your petrol level topped up you'll break down because you've run out of fuel. But even putting this aside, it's a good idea not to let the level drop too low. 'Any particles of dirt and sediment accumulate at the bottom of the fuel tank so driving it until there isn't much left means that all this gunk gets pushed through the fuel system,' says Vanessa Guyll. 'Filling up when there's still a quarter of a tank left means you'll be using cleaner fuel, which is better for your car.'

Planning ahead also means you'll have more time to shop around for cheaper fuel.

How

Filling up at your local garage is usually quite straightforward. It's important to remember where on the car your fuel cap is so you can pull up with that side closest to the pump. If you have problems with getting the fuel cap back on then most garages sell rubber replacement ones to tide you over.

Don't smoke or use your mobile near the pump as both are dangerous.

O – oil

Why

Oil lubricates the moving parts within the engine and prevents corrosion. If the level drops too low then there will be a lot of wear and tear on the poor old engine and it could seize up, causing serious and expensive damage. Once they're run in, new cars don't often need more oil between services, though older cars are more likely to. But it's important to check anyway, as if the level has dropped suddenly this means there's a leak which will need to be investigated.

How

The driver's manual will show you where the oil dipstick is. You'll need to pull the dipstick out and wipe it with a clean cloth or bit of kitchen roll, then put it all the way back in again. Then remove it and check the dipstick. There will be a maximum and minimum level marked on it and the oil mark should be between these two lines.

If the oil does need topping up, then look in your manual for the place it has to go. Rather confusingly, this won't be where the dipstick is – there will be a different cap, often with a picture of a dripping oil can on it, which you'll need to remove. Don't go sloshing any old oil into your car though. These days cars tend to require oils which are 'engine specific' – you'll need to look in your manual to see what you should be using. It's also important to know what oil has been used in the car before –

for example, if it's got long-life oil in it then adding ordinary oil can interact badly with it and destroy its special properties. Once you've got the right product, pour in a little oil through a funnel – don't overdo it, as overfilling can be damaging too. Then wait a few seconds for it to settle and check it again with the dipstick.

If the oil level drops unexpectedly it may well indicate a leak. If you suspect this then inspect the ground underneath the vehicle for stains and check the level again the following day – if there's another drop then take your car to a garage.

W – windscreen washer and other fluid levels

Windscreen washer fluid

Why
This is one level that will drop in the normal course of events – the washer fluid gets used up every time you do that squirty thing to clean your windscreen. If it runs out then you'll be stuck with a dirty screen and visibility will be a problem, especially in foggy or sunny conditions.

How
Locate the windscreen washer container using the car handbook – it's often got an image of jets of water on the cap. It will have maximum and minimum levels marked on the side of the transparent plastic container. You should be able to see through it to view the level of fluid. If it's low then top it up with a mixture of water and screen wash. Don't use washing-up liquid whatever you do as it foams up too much and will give you a smeary windscreen. Also, proper screen wash contains chemicals to prevent the fluid turning into a block of ice in winter.

It's important to check the nozzles where the spray comes

out as they can easily get clogged up. If that happens then clean the gunk away using something pointy like a needle.

Coolant

Why

The coolant is a mixture of water and antifreeze that is used in the car's cooling system. It stops your engine from overheating or freezing and prevents the engine corroding.

How

The coolant is stored in a transparent plastic container. Sometimes this is referred to as 'the radiator' but in modern cars the actual radiator itself will be tucked away and the coolant runs down into it.

Check that the fluid level is between the maximum and minimum levels. If it's below the minimum then take a cloth, carefully remove the cap and add some water – don't bother with antifreeze as there are lots of different types and mixing them can cause problems. This is a job best left for your garage, who should check the water:antifreeze ratio when the car goes in for a service and adjust it accordingly. Coolant shouldn't need much topping up and if it does then it's likely there's a problem with the engine that needs sorting out – so it's another take-it-to-a-garage scenario.

The other fluids

In addition to the above your car will also have a container for brake fluid and may have others such as power steering and clutch fluid. Again, these can be checked visually through the container wall. Avoid opening the brake fluid container in particular as it degrades when it comes into contact with air. None of these fluid levels should drop in the normal course of events.

If they do there's a problem that you should refer to a trained mechanic.

D – damage (check for any damage to the car)

Windows, glass and bodywork

Why

Windscreen chips are particularly important to spot early, before they develop into a full-blown crack. Side mirrors are also vital to check. If they've been damaged or got a crack in them then they could fall out at any moment – and you certainly don't want that happening when you're bombing down the slip road for the M25.

It's also important to check for signs of rust so this can be treated early.

How

Walk round your car and give it the once-over. If you spot a chip or crack in your glass then Autoglass (www.autoglass.co.uk; 0800 587 8198) or one of the other specialist glass companies will be able to come to your home or work and repair it for a reasonable price. It's worth checking with your insurance company to see if they'll cover the cost for you – many fully comprehensive policies do.

Broken side mirrors and rust are both problems you can take to a garage or that you might want to tackle yourself (see the 'Grease monkey' section on p. 85 for more details).

E – electrics (lights) and battery

Lights

Why

It's important to have working lights so you can see in the dark, and show other drivers that you're braking or taking a particular turning or roundabout exit.

How

It's easiest to check your lights after dark and with a helper – that way you can be at the wheel operating the various switches and the helper can run around making sure they're coming on properly.

- ⊖ Start your car, put it in neutral and put the handbrake on.
- ⊖ Turn the headlights full on.
- ⊖ Open both doors and check your lights as follows:

  two headlamps – on regular and high beam
  left and right side lights
  left and right rear lights.

- ⊖ Check the indicators individually, not just by turning on the hazard warning switch, which is usually on a different circuit – if there's a wiring fault with the indicators this might not be revealed by the hazard warning lights.
- ⊖ Switch on your left-turn indicator – confirm both front and rear left indicator lights are flashing.
- ⊖ Do the same for the right-turn indicator.
- ⊖ Put the car in reverse and check the white reversing lights.
- ⊖ Finally put the car back in neutral and step on the brake lights. Check that the red brake lights come on.

Many modern cars have light emitting diodes (LEDs) instead of bulbs in the side and brake lights and indicators. These should last the life of the car, but sometimes they do go wrong and you'll need to have them repaired at a garage.

If any of the bulbs have failed they'll need to be replaced. One option is to take the car to a garage, another is to use Halfords' We-Fit service (see p. 75). For older cars buying the relevant bulb and doing it yourself is possible, though it can be a bit fiddly. For newer cars the space under the bonnet is so cramped that access can be very difficult, so getting it done by a mechanic will be your best option.

In theory I can replace a headlight bulb but it's easier to take it to the garage and they can have the challenge of fiddling with tiny wires behind the glove compartment. Anjali, 28

Battery

Why
Battery failure is one of the main causes of breakdowns.

How
Most car batteries these days are 'maintenance-free' which means dismantling them and doing stuff like 'topping up the electrolyte levels' is no longer required, thank goodness. To be honest, anything to do with the battery should be approached with extreme caution. They can give you a nasty electric shock, the fluid in them is a very powerful acid and they contain lead so they're very heavy to remove from the car. It's a good idea not to tackle anything to do with your battery, not even taking it out and recharging it until you've had some proper instruction or been on a car maintenance course.

However, if there are signs that your battery is playing up (for example, the car is slow to start in the morning) you can take it to a garage who will put a meter on it to check that the charge is OK. Many garages have signs offering free battery checks – the reasoning being that if there is a problem with it then you're on the spot for them to try to flog you a new one. For this reason it's a good idea to say you want to learn more about your car and ask if you can watch as they use the meter. That way you can see if the needle really goes into the red or not! Sometimes it's enough to recharge a failing battery, but at other times you'll need a new one.

Batteries need to get replaced about every four years and though some show signs of ill health beforehand, others just pack up one day without warning. They get run down by having lots of equipment run off them (lights, in-car DVD players, etc.), so don't have things running if it's not necessary (for example, turn off the heated rear screen once it has done its job and charge your phone up at home before you set off). The reason why batteries tend to fail more in winter is that they've got more electrical stuff like headlamps and heating running off them at that time of year. Doing lots of short journeys will run it down too – but a good twenty-minute clear drive every so often will help keep it charged up.

R – rubber (tyres and windscreen wipers)

Tyres

Why

Because if your tyres are damaged, don't have enough tread or aren't inflated properly you're far more likely to get a puncture and be left stranded at the side of the road. This will probably happen when you're on the way to an important meeting, a hot date or your best friend's wedding. Or when you've got two fractious children in the back. And of course, if you get a puncture when you're driving at a high speed it can be very dangerous.

Having your tyres inflated to the correct pressure also makes for maximum fuel efficiency and will help keep your motoring as cheap and green as possible.

How
You'll find the correct tyre pressures for your particular car in your car handbook – often they advise different pressures for the front and rear tyres or for when the car is heavily laden. It's worth making a note of them in your diary or putting a memo in the glove compartment so you've always got them close to hand. Some cars have their tyre pressure inscribed on the inside of the fuel cap.

Tyre pressures need to be checked when the tyre is cold, so you should either do it at home or at a petrol station that's less than a mile away. If the pressure is too low then you'll need to inflate them. The petrol station forecourt machines can both check your tyre pressures and provide air if necessary. But you can also buy gadgets to check and inflate them (via a foot or electrical pump) at home. The latter can be particularly useful if you live some distance from your local garage or just don't like faffing about on the forecourt.

> *I used to hate checking my tyre pressures at my local petrol station. Because I'm young any older blokes around would assume I was clueless and come over to help and I'd get flustered. But I bought a combined tyre pressure checker and foot pump and now I do it on our front drive – it's so much easier.* Adele, 17

You should also check the pressure in your spare tyre – though that can be a drag if it's in the boot and you have to haul everything out to get at it. A useful gadget in this instance is Pirtek's 'Air in Your Spare Kit', which costs about £15 from independent spares retailers. It's a flexible hose that fits onto the valve of your spare tyre, and which you can then route up into the main boot area and attach to the side wall with velcro straps. The pressure gauge on the end of the flexible hose will show when the pressure has fallen too low in the spare tyre.

If one tyre is significantly more down than the others be aware that it might have a slow puncture. One way of checking is to lick your finger and put saliva across the valve and see if the leaking air forms a bubble. Another is to check the pressure again the following day – if it's down again that quickly then there's definitely a problem.

It's also important to check your tyres for damage and to make sure the tread depth is OK. Have a look at them to see that they haven't got any nails or bits of gravel in them. Then check the tread depth – you can do this with a tyre-depth gauge, which is cheap and readily available from somewhere like Halfords. The legal minimum is 1.6 mm, but really it should be 3 mm or more. The average new tyre tends to come with about 8 mm of tread but performance deteriorates rapidly in the second half of its life and it can go from being absolutely fine to dangerously low quite quickly. How long a tyre lasts depends very much on the car, the particular type of tyre and your driving style, but they should last on average for 30,000 miles.

'Because the roads are in a poor state it's easy for your steering alignment to get knocked out,' says Adam Ashmore, top breakdown patrolman at the AA. 'Then tyres can start getting worn in odd places very quickly. It's worrying how many people are driving round on dangerous and illegal tyres.'

If your tyres are damaged or the tread is too thin then you'll have to have them replaced. This could be done at your garage though your local tyre-fitting specialist will probably be your cheapest option – phone around for quotes.

Windscreen wiper blades

Why

Around 20 per cent of accidents are caused by poor visibility and if your wiper blades are getting old and worn they won't be able to clean the screen properly. If they show signs of wear and tear or have been leaving smears on the windscreen, it's time to change them.

How

You could take your car to a garage or use Halfords' We-Fit service (see p. 75) but this is actually one of those car-related tasks that it's reasonably easy to do yourself. There's a helpful demonstration video at www.carparts-direct.co.uk that you might like to check out.

Grease monkey

Once you feel confident doing the checks you might like to consider doing simple repairs yourself or even servicing your own car. As has been mentioned earlier, this will be easier if you've got an older car, but you can still do external stuff such as repairing scratches or rust on newer ones.

But don't just plunge recklessly in at the deep end. A 'have a go' attitude is an admirable thing in many areas of life, but when it comes to doing work on a metal box destined to carry you at 70 m.p.h., a more cautious approach is advisable. There are certain items you really don't want to go anywhere near unless you know what you're doing. They include the brakes, battery, cam-belt, spark plugs and the cooling system.

It's also worth bearing in mind that repairing your car will involve some initial investment. It's a bit like taking up carpentry as a hobby – you'll need to buy or borrow the right tools. The best way to get started is to join a car maintenance class. That way you'll receive expert guidance and also get a feel for whether it's something you want to pursue.

I took an Introduction to Car Mechanics course at my local college. The tutor was really great and now I can do basic repairs and service my own car. I'm a single parent on a tight budget and doing my own repairs has made the difference between my being able to run a car or having to do without one. Nuala, 33

Chapter 5

The Girls' Guide to Garages

No matter how much you care for your car, there are going to be times when you'll have to take it to a garage. With luck, it won't need repairs very often, but it will definitely need servicing at intervals and if it's over three years old then an annual MOT (Ministry of Transport) test is a legal requirement. So a vital part of car ownership is to find a good garage – one that you can trust and which will deal with you honestly rather than rip you off.

This can pose something of a challenge, to put it mildly. Personal recommendation has always been seen as the best approach when looking for a decent garage, and it's definitely an important factor. But because there are different types of garages (franchised dealerships, independents, specialized fitting centres, etc.), it means that one meeting someone else's needs might not fit your particular requirements.

For example, if your friend has a much-loved old Peugeot that her helpful local garage keeps on the road, that's great. But if you're driving a new Hyundai that is under warranty then it's advisable to have it repaired and serviced by the Hyundai dealership in order to keep the warranty up to date. The different types of warranty, what they cover and how to keep them valid are covered in detail in Chapter 8, 'Gotta New Motor?' However, when the warranty expires you can then make a decision about whether you stay with the dealership (which is likely to be more expensive) or change to an independent garage. If you decide to go for the latter this is the point at which your friend's recommendation will come in useful.

Garages are not created equal

The first thing to know about garages is that they're not created equal – there are different types, each with its pros and cons. Here are your main options and what you can expect from them.

Franchised dealership

A franchised dealership is one that is linked to a particular manufacturer, such as BMW or Nissan. They usually have a car salesroom, a workshop for repairs and servicing and a parts department in the same premises. But if you bought your car from a particular dealership, it doesn't mean you have to take it back there for servicing and repairs. If another garage in the same franchise is more convenient for you, or if you've heard positive reports of it, then go there instead. Costs can also vary even within the same franchise so it's worth shopping around to find the best value.

Dealerships usually have quite an upmarket feel. You get a plush-carpeted reception area, pot plants, aquariums, glossy magazines lying around and so forth. If you want to keep as much distance as possible between yourself and the gritty, grimy side of motoring then this is where you'll feel most comfortable. On arrival you'll get to explain your problem and hand your keys over to some glamorous blonde receptionist and your car will be whisked away to be worked on by unseen mechanics.

Some dealerships offer a collection service, so you might not even have to go to the garage, and most offer a courtesy car for you to use while your car is being worked on. But if you do have to hang around while they complete a job the reception area is usually reasonably pleasant to wait in.

> *My Citroën had a problem with the boot opening. I had to go back three times before they finally managed to fix it but there was a coffee shop there and I was able to work on my laptop while they were fiddling about, so it wasn't too bad.* Clare, 32

Franchised dealers also have the most up-to-date diagnostic equipment, receive special updates from the manufacturer about any changes or problems with particular cars and all the mechanics are trained to work on your particular make of vehicle. However, they do tend to be significantly more expensive than independent garages.

Independent garage

There are unlikely to be posh carpets or a waiting area in your average independent garage. Instead you'll probably have to loiter in the doorway calling out 'Hello? Hello?' until a bloke in a grimy overall appears and then explain your problem over the background noise of someone welding and a radio playing Chris Moyles at full blast. But the positive side of this is that you often get to speak directly to the person who'll be working on your car and are able to explain the precise nature of the odd rattling noise it has been making.

Independent garages can be very good, very bad and all points in between – this is where personal recommendations really come into their own. If you find a trustworthy one and use it regularly then there's the chance to build a solid personal relationship where they really get to know you and your car.

Specialized fitting centres

These specialize in certain items such as tyres, exhausts, shock absorbers and batteries. They often offer far better deals on tyres than either franchised dealers or independents and can provide good value on other items. If you're not happy with the price offered by your usual garage for providing and fitting these parts it's worth getting a quote from a specialized fitting centre. And if you phone another centre and mention that quote then they'll probably offer to undercut it – if haggling is your thing then you can make significant savings.

Specialist fitting centres are usually located out of town on industrial estates, and do the work while you wait. The reception and waiting facilities tend to be pretty basic but the service is usually brisk and it's unlikely that you'll be kept hanging around for long. They tend to work on a 'menu pricing' basis – where you pay a set rate for, say, fitting a clutch. This means that whether the job is done quickly or whether a technical problem comes up which means it takes longer, you still pay the same price.

Breaking down the costs

The cost of having work done on your car breaks down into:

The cost of parts and 'consumables'

The parts are the actual items the garage replaces on your car, such as a new battery or headlamps. Some will be referred to as 'original parts' – that means they're made by Skoda or Audi or whoever. Then there are cheaper versions of the same thing, commonly called 'parts of equivalent quality' (if they're seen as being very good) or 'substitute parts'. It's a bit like inkjet printer cartridges – if you've got a Hewlett Packard printer you might want to use HP cartridges in it, or cheaper ones sold by another company, which may or may not be as good.

Franchised dealers will always use the more expensive original parts and generally guarantee them for a year. If you're using an independent you may be offered a choice of original or substitute parts and the time they're guaranteed will vary.

'Consumables' are items like oil and screen wash.

Labour rates

This covers the mechanics' wages and general overheads, which are significantly higher at franchised dealers than independents. A survey by warranty specialists Warranty Direct in 2005 investigating labour rates at franchised and independent garages came up with the following findings:

In London the average franchised dealer hourly labour rate was £98, while the average for independent garages was £64.

In Cardiff the similar rates were £84 and £42, in Newcastle they were £72 and £31.

The labour rates also varied between dealerships, with a maximum hourly rate of £129 charged by a Land Rover garage, £116 by a Porsche dealer and £89 by a Nissan dealership.

How long they take to do the job

But you've also got to factor in how long your chosen garage might take to do the job. If the franchised dealer completes it quicker because they've got the right equipment then it'll work out cheaper even though the labour rates are higher. But then, on the other hand, they tend to use more apprentices on their teams, whilst independent garages will have experienced mechanics. As you can see, it can all get quite complicated.

Menu pricing

Many franchised garages and independents offer a 'menu pricing' system similar to that offered at specialized fitting centres where you pay a flat rate for a particular job, regardless of how long it takes them.

When all the different factors are taken into consideration independent garages on the whole work out significantly cheaper than going to a franchised dealer. To give an example, the consumer organization Which? ran a survey in July 2007 in which it found that average service prices worked out at £255 at a franchised dealership and £166 at an independent garage – about £89 cheaper overall.

The franchised dealer vs independent garage debate

If your car is under warranty then it's best to use a franchised dealership for servicing and repairs. Although it's technically possible to take it to an independent garage for servicing (provided that parts of equivalent quality are used and the manufacturer's procedures are followed) it's a bit of a legal grey area and it's probably best not to give the manufacturer any opportunity to declare the warranty invalid. Any necessary repairs of warranty items under the warranty period should of course be carried out by the dealer free of charge.

Another reason to take a new or newish car to the dealer for servicing is because an FDSH (full dealer service history) is seen as a desirable thing which will make the car more attractive to buyers when and if you come to sell it. Also, if you're loyal about having your car serviced at the dealership there's the possibility that they might knock something off the cost of any future repairs. 'If a problem develops shortly after the warranty expires then it's worth asking the garage to submit a "post-warranty claim" and seeing if the manufacturer will cover or at least subsidize certain repairs,' says Vanessa Guyll of the AA. 'Some dealers are exceptionally good and will do this for a number of years afterwards.' The dealer's only involvement is sending off the paperwork – the decision is made by the manufacturer.

However, David Evans, motoring specialist at consumer organization Which?, has doubts about the value of using a franchised dealership. 'Franchised dealerships tend to be about 35 per cent more expensive than independent garages and our surveys have shown that there's no guarantee that you're buying competence with the extra money. I also think that the issue of having an FDSH for resale value has been over-rated.' David is also sceptical about the possibility of post-warranty claims. 'If there's a part in your car which the manufacturer says should last for ten years and it packs up after five, there's a chance they might contribute to the cost of fixing it. But this is only at their own discretion and in my experience it's so rare for them to cough up that it's not worth sticking with the franchise for.'

So, as you can see, there's an ongoing debate about the value of sticking with a franchised dealership after the warranty has run out. Asking around among family and friends will help you decide when to move on to an independent – most people seem to drift off to one a year or so after their warranty has expired.

Don't get taken for a ride

The Big Question in almost every girl's mind when dealing with a garage is – am I going to get hugely ripped off here? And the answer to it is – yes, you might be. 'It's hard enough finding a good plumber or builder, but we think it's even harder to find a garage you can really trust to service and repair your car,' says David Evans of Which?. 'As our undercover investigations have shown over the years, slack practices and overcharging are rife in this business and you need to choose your garage with care.'

In July 2007 *Which?* magazine carried out a garage survey. They took fifty cars, all within their new-car warranty, to garages around the country for a service. They had created some small faults in some of the cars and wanted to check if these had been spotted, and also if unnecessary work was carried out. The results don't exactly inspire confidence:

⊖ For example, the *Which?* team deliberately blew one of the reversing light bulbs – but this fault was missed by 25 out of the 50 garages.

- One of the tyre pressures was 20 per cent less than it should have been, and this was missed by 9 out of the 50 garages.
- *Which?* also filled up all the cars with screen wash before taking them in – but 20 out of the 50 garages charged for topping it up, even though it was already full.

Here are some examples of other scams used by dishonest garages:

- Charging two hours' labour for a job which really only took them an hour.
- Using a cheap brand of oil but charging you for the top-of-the-range variety.
- Spraying oil on your shock absorber and telling you that it's leaking.
- Telling you that the cost of repairs to your vehicle is more than it's worth and then trying to flog you a car from their forecourt. Driving past a few weeks later you're likely to see your 'irreparable' car tarted up and for sale at a tidy price.
- Saying that your clutch was damaged and they had to replace it but actually not doing anything at all.

MOT time is when dishonest mechanics can really start rubbing their hands together and cackling! Most people are worried that their car will need expensive repairs and be pleased if the cost of getting it through is fairly modest. So even if your car is in tip-top condition the garage will know that it can probably fabricate a hundred pounds or so of work and, far from cross-examining them about it, you'll be so relieved it's not more you'll happily pay up.

Some people will give you strategies for trying to catch out slippery garages – but most are either impractical (unless you stand over someone with a stopwatch you're going to have to take on trust how long a particular job took) or require a level of mechanical knowledge that most of us just don't have.

> *A colleague warned me that if a garage was going to replace something on my car I should ask them to keep the old part and show it to me, so I could be sure they'd really done it. But I've also heard that dodgy garages have got wind of this strategy and keep a supply of old parts that they'll wave in front of customers to keep them happy. And I know so little about cars anyway, they could hand me something and say 'this is your clutch' and it could actually be a bit out of an old washing machine and I wouldn't know the difference.* Kerry, 20

Basically, if a garage is determined to behave dishonestly then it will – and if it's not able to bump up its bill via one method, then it'll do it by another. So in much the same way that it's more sensible to dump a cheating boyfriend rather than waste your time trying to purloin his phone so you can check for incriminating messages, it's also wiser to just avoid garages that you suspect might be trying to put one over on you. Far better to channel your energy into finding a garage (and indeed, a man) you can trust.

There are plenty of good garages out there – you just have to be prepared to put in a bit of legwork to track them down. It's also important not to just judge on price – it's worth paying a bit more to get a reliable and helpful garage.

Personal recommendation

As has been mentioned previously, personal recommendation is the best way to find a good garage. Asking around friends, family, work colleagues and on car-related motoring forums will help point you in the right direction. It's also worth bearing in mind that garages in rural areas can be better than those in towns as they'll be particularly concerned about their reputation.

> *I live in a small retirement town in Devon and all the local garages are good – they wouldn't dare not to be! Gossip spreads like wildfire round here and if any tradesman got caught out trying to rip someone off he'd have all the local Women's Institutes marching on his workshop carrying pitchforks and flaming torches.* Julia, 55

It's good not to become over-dependent on a particular garage however.

> *I live in Glasgow but I always have my MOT done when I go back home to Peterborough. A friend of my dad's runs a garage and we've always used him – I wouldn't trust anyone else not to rip me off.* Salma, 27

Such loyalty is touching, but doesn't necessarily make good financial sense. It's important to have someone local you can rely on in case you need emergency repairs – so if you move somewhere new start asking around as soon as possible.

Membership of a trade association

Anyone can open an independent garage and start trading – it's not necessary to have any formal qualifications. So if you use a garage where the mechanics are trained, certificates are displayed and they are a member of a recognized body such as the Retail Motor Industry Federation then that is at least a start.

- The Motor Vehicles Repairers Association, www.mvra.co.uk. Call 0870 458 3051 for details of member garages in your area.
- The Retail Motor Industry Federation, www.rmif.co.uk, has a search facility for local members or you can phone them on 0845 758 5350.
- The Scottish Motor Trade Association, www.smta.co.uk, 0131 331 5510.

Membership of a 'good garage' scheme

Some garages choose to join various 'good garage schemes'. These are organizations that promote their members but also require certain standards of them, which, if not maintained, will mean the member will be disqualified. Many of these schemes offer a complaints procedure for customers. The fact that a garage has gone to the trouble to join one of these schemes is promising and shows the right attitude – so you might like to research members of the following ones in your area.

Bosch car service network

This is a scheme that independent garages can join – the deal is that the garage will work to certain standards and in return they'll get the benefit of gaining new customers as a result of their membership. Bosch audits all the member garages and uses mystery shoppers to check standards are maintained. It's the only scheme currently recognized by the Office of Fair Trading. There are over 400 garages in the network and to find the one that's nearest to you check out their website at www.boschcarservice.co.uk.

Motor Industry Code

This is a new scheme developed by the motor industry to create a network of garages that customers can trust. Garages that join the Code are agreeing to keep to certain standards such as an open and honest pricing system and a straightforward complaints procedure. And if you're not happy with their service then a free advice line is available. Their website at www.motorindustrycodes.co.uk will let you know of garages in your area which subscribe to the Code or call 0800 692 0825.

Foxy Lady Drivers

The Foxy Lady Drivers' club costs £20 to join and offers individual advice on motoring matters via email and has an approved list of female-friendly garages. For more details check out www.foxyladydrivers.com or call 01903 879 988.

Some other ways to find a good garage

Which? Local website

This website helps members share information about local tradespeople. Currently there are 1200 garages throughout the country recommended on www.which-local. co.uk. All recommendations are checked by Which? to make sure they're above board and that the person posting them doesn't have a personal connection with the garage.

You need to be a Which? subscriber to use this website, but they do publish their annual list of the best garages in the UK – if one of these is near you then they'd be worth trying.

Which? Local Top Five Garages, January 2009

Northwood Auto Services, Northwood, Middlesex
Wheelbase Garage Ltd, Walton on Thames, Surrey

RJ Auto Services, Bromley, Kent
FMS Car and Truck, Stafford
JK Auto Services, Woolwich, London

Top Technicans 2008

The annual Top Technician award is run by a group of leading motor trade associations, including the IMI: The Institute of the Motor Industry and the ATA: Automotive Technician Accreditation. If you live near any of these guys then one of them could be the right mechanic for you.

In 2008 the winner of the Top Technician award was Mark Banks of Holmer Green Service Centre, High Wycombe, Buckinghamshire, with Kim Doerr of DD Auto Services, Flitwick, Bedfordshire and Stephen Martin of Cooper BMW, Norwich as runners-up.

The other finalists were

Jerry Carroll of Carroll's Garage, Paisley, Renfrewshire
Mark Chandler of Sherlodge Garage, Gillingham, Kent
Peter Duncombe of County Fleet Maintenance, Birmingham
Jason Evans of Cotswold BMW, Hereford, Herefordshire
Phil Huelin of Goodwin's Garage, St Helier, Jersey
David Wagstaff of D. C. Mardles Motor Engineers, Exeter
Paul Williams of Enterprise Garage, Arundel, West Sussex
Keith Windle of Skipton Ford Mazda, Skipton, North
Yorkshire
Dan Wright of Clive Atthowe Tuning, Norwich, Norfolk

Could this be the start of a beautiful relationship?

Hopefully the various routes outlined above will prove useful and help you narrow down your search to a few potential garages. Once you've done that it's time to investigate further.

Like any relationship, it's best if you can get to know each other gradually rather than plunge in at the deep end. So in an ideal scenario it would be wise to just have a few minor bits of work done first – maybe a headlight bulb change or a service. That way you can get a general feel for the place and suss out how friendly and reliable they are and whether they appear to be dealing fairly with you. Of course, this isn't always possible. For example if you've just moved to a new area and your car needs major repairs urgently. But under normal circumstances it's good if you can take things slowly.

It's a bit like trying out a new hairdresser – you'd probably go in for a trim or maybe a few highlights first and check out the way the hairdresser worked before asking to have your waist-length chestnut hair transformed into a blonde urchin cut.

Hanging on the telephone

It's a good idea to phone a couple of garages on your shortlist and have an initial chat with them.

When talking to different garages always make sure you compare like with like. Services in particular are an area where vagueness can prevail. When garages talk about 'doing a service' they can be referring to a procedure that's as brisk as an oil and filter change or one that involves a thorough check of the car and replacing loads of important stuff like spark plugs and brake pads. So it's important to be clear about what you're actually getting. Services are covered in full in the following chapter.

If you're describing a problem with your car, it's important to be as specific as possible about what happens and when the problem occurs. For example – 'there's a scraping noise when I brake' or 'there's a blowing noise when I accelerate'.

Ask about how long they think the work might take and when they might be able to book you in for it. Ask them what their hourly labour rate is and what sort of parts they might use on your car. When discussing prices it's important to be aware of whether you're being given an estimate or a quote. Quotes should be supplied in writing and cover exactly what the garage plans to do and give a definite price for the work. Estimates are a rough idea of what the garage thinks it will cost. Also ask them whether the figures they're quoting include or exclude VAT – you don't want to go for one that sounds like a good deal and then realize it's only because they left VAT off!

Taking your car into the garage

It's important to be punctual if you've booked to bring your car in at a particular time – being late could mess up their work schedule and it's important to deal with the garage as fairly as you'd like them to deal with you. Make sure your car has enough fuel in it as they might need to take it for a test drive to check out any problems. It's worth making a note where the gauge is, however, as some naughty garages will use cars in for work as their personal runarounds and if they use up a lot of your fuel you'll know to avoid them in future.

If possible, don't drop your car off when you're in a rush, especially if it's your first visit to an independent garage. Talk your requirements over with the garage manager or mechanic and get a feel for the general vibe of the place. Are they friendly and happy to explain things? Or do they respond to questions by giving you the brush-off? This is an area where feminine intuition can come in particularly useful.

My rule is – never leave your car with a garage where the mechanic doesn't look you in the eye when he's discussing costs. Anjali, 28

If you get the chance to discuss your car problem with family, friends or colleagues beforehand, then do so – that way you can say stuff like, 'my friend thinks it might be worn brake pads' or 'my dad thinks there's a problem with the starter motor'. It will at least let them know you've got knowledgeable people in your social circle and that you're not totally a poor defenceless female all alone in the world. That can feel a bit like cheating for those of us who take a 'girls can do anything and we don't need to rely on a bloke' approach to life, but there you go.

Even if you feel a bit out of your depth, avoid playing the 'helpless female' card. 'Be confident and don't go on about how little you know,' says Vanessa Guyll of the AA. 'Ask questions and show you're open to learning more about your car.' This is a time to mention any particular requirements. For example, if they're going to be doing anything to the wheels and you want to be able to change them yourself then ask them not to tighten the nuts too much.

If there's any uncertainty about how much the work might cost, agree a price and ask them not to go above it without calling you first. Ask for an itemized bill and agree a collection time.

Post-match analysis

It's best to pick up your car when you're not on a tight schedule. That way you'll be able to have a talk with the mechanic or service manager. Ask them to go through the list of what they've done with you. If a tyre was replaced, for example, then ask why. Was it damage or a poor tread? If you're uncomfortable that this might come across as though you're checking up on them (though this is of course exactly what you're doing!) say that you're trying to learn more about your car. Phrasing it that way will make for a more positive vibe.

Many garages hold back the parts they've removed and will show or offer to give them to you. It can feel a bit odd going off with a plastic bag with some dusty brake pads in it, but it is worth doing as it's all part of the learning curve. Once you get back home, open the bonnet and look the car over – you should be able to see where they've done work because the area should be cleaner.

If the work involved disturbing any gaskets or seals park the car overnight with a sheet of card or paper underneath or pick a clean bit of road or driveway. Then you can check for signs of leaks in the morning – if there are any, take the car back to the garage and explain what's happened.

Discuss what you had done and how much it cost you with family, friends and colleagues and see if they nod approvingly or splutter out their coffee and squawk about how you've been robbed.

With luck you'll find a fantastic garage and can start settling into a long-term relationship – but if you're not happy with how your initial visit has gone then try another one next time. There are some great, good-value garages out there and you'll find one in the end!

If you need to complain

Contact the garage – speak to the receptionist or garage manager as soon as you can and give them a chance to put things right – ideally they should get any problems sorted at this stage.

If not, it's worth calling Consumer Direct, a division of the Office of Fair Trading on 08454 040 506 to get an idea of what next step is best for your particular situation. You might also want to get in touch with your local Citizens Advice Bureau. They might suggest that you try the manufacturer if it's a franchised dealership – they should have a formal procedure for dealing with complaints.

If it's an independent garage then contact any professional body they belong to, or if they're a member of the Bosch or Foxy Lady Drivers schemes then give them a call.

If the situation is really escalating then it's worth getting in touch with Which? Legal. They've got a scheme that costs £15 a quarter whereby you'll be able to call up a legal adviser who will give you advice, help you write a suitable letter, etc. You don't have to be a member of Which? to use this service.

Chapter 6

Services, MOTs and Repairs

Services, MOTs and repairs are the three main things you're likely to get done at a garage. Here's an outline of what they'll probably involve so you can discuss them confidently with your mechanic – or at least bluff your way through!

Services

What's a service and why does my car need one?

Cars are complicated machines. Over time, and through being driven, various mechanical bits get worn, the fluids used to lubricate the car get dirty or used up, and various items need to be replaced. The purpose of a service is to offset all this wear and tear by making sure that at intervals stuff gets checked and if necessary changed and the car is generally primed up.

Regular services will make your car last longer, be safer to drive, more fuel-efficient and better for the environment. A service record proving that this work has been carried out will also help your car retain its value and be easier to sell. Of course one possible outcome of having things checked is that a problem might be uncovered – but it's better to find this out during a service than to only realize that you've got a problem with your exhaust when it drops off as you're hurtling along the motorway.

What needs doing and how often?

Like garages, not all services are created equal. Every manufacturer outlines a service schedule for each of its models, saying what checks and changes should happen and when they should take place. You'll usually find this information in the service record book that will have been supplied when the car was new. If you've got a second-hand car and the service record book has been mislaid along the way then you should be able to get one from an authorized dealer.

The type of things that get done at different points do of course vary, but here are some rough guidelines just to give you an idea.

A basic service (usually annually or every 10,000 miles, whichever is soonest) generally involves:

- ☺ Changing the engine oil and filter.
- ☺ Changing the air filter (this filters the dirt out of the air before the air goes into the engine).
- ☺ Changing the cabin pollen filter (this filters the particles out of the air before it goes into the 'cabin' of the car – the bit where everyone sits).
- ☺ Lubricating the door hinges and locks.
- ☺ Checking the coolant, screen wash, brake fluid and power-steering fluid levels.
- ☺ Checking the concentration of antifreeze.

⊛ Checking the condition of the windscreen wipers.

⊛ Checking the lights and horn.

⊛ Checking the brakes.

A full service (usually every two years or every 20,000 miles) does all of the above plus:

⊛ Draining and replacing the brake fluid.

⊛ Replacing brake pads (and discs if needed).

⊛ Replacing spark plugs.

⊛ Checking the engine ancillary drive belts and replacing if necessary.

⊛ Checking and servicing the air-conditioning system.

Extra checks and changes

Cam-belt (also known as the timing belt)

Replacing the cam-belt. This lasts about 40,000 miles on older cars but with new ones it will last much longer. However, it's important not to forget about it – if this belt snaps it's goodbye engine!

Battery

The battery will probably need replacing every four years or so – more frequently if you do lots of short journeys.

Draining and replacing the antifreeze/coolant mixture

This happens every four or five years.

What will your service cover?

As mentioned in Chapter 2, when you're booking in for a service you need to know exactly what you're getting. With newer cars it's important to follow the manufacturer's schedule to help the car retain its resale value.

Increasingly, garages are using a 'service checklist' – a standard printed form with all the things they could possibly do listed on it, and the ones they've actually done checked off. Ask if they use one of these and if you can have one – it'll also come in useful if you take the car to another garage, as they'll be able to see at a glance the work that's been done recently.

As the car gets very old and you think it might be about to give up on you anyway, you might want to skimp on a few things rather than spend money cosseting an elderly car. However, some people become even more attentive as their motor gets older as they don't want to lose it – it's a personal choice and one you can talk over with your garage and with family and friends.

Timing of the services

If your car is still under warranty you've got to be very on the ball about having the services done at the right time and in accordance with the manufacturer's schedule. If you're not, the warranty can be declared invalid and you'll have to pay for any repairs yourself. Be sure to mark the date they're due in your diary and book your car in well in advance.

Most people are conscientious about servicing when their car is new but as it gets older it can become one of those things that you let slide. That isn't a good idea at all though – regular servicing, whether that's very thorough or a more basic oil and filter change is essential for all cars, regardless of their age.

As a car gets older, how it's driven will also influence how often it needs to be serviced – for example, lots of short journeys where the engine doesn't have a chance to warm up properly will probably mean that more frequent oil and filter changes are needed.

Some cars like those from the VW group and BMW have sophisticated service indicators which take data on how the car is used, and adjust the service intervals accordingly – so a light on the dashboard might indicate that after another 500 miles the oil needs changing or whatever.

A good time to have your car serviced is just before the MOT, so that if the car has any problems it'll flag up some (but not necessarily all) of them and give you a chance to put them right.

Once the service has been completed it's important to get the service book stamped.

The MOT

In the UK all cars over three years old are legally required to undergo an annual MOT test. This test was introduced in 1960 and is a compulsory examination of key mechanical and electrical points to ensure that the car is still basically roadworthy and that any faults or potential problems can be sorted out.

MOTs are now registered on a central database so the police and insurance companies can check that any car has a valid certificate. You can't tax a car without an MOT, and insurance may be invalid if you don't have one. It's also against the law to drive a car with an out-of-date MOT certificate unless you are driving it to or from an MOT test centre with a booked appointment.

The MOT is coordinated by the Vehicle Operator Services Agency (VOSA) and you can learn more about them and find local test centres on their website at www.vosa.gov.uk.

When does it need doing?

You can get your MOT carried out from one month before the expiry date of the old certificate. It's always a good idea to take the plunge and have it done as soon as possible. Any new MOT certificate will still be dated for a year from the end of the old one, so you don't lose any time from it by getting in early. And if it fails it'll give you extra time to investigate the best place to have repairs done before re-submitting it for another test or to consider your options if you decide to sell or scrap your car.

Where should I have it done?

There are about 19,000 MOT testing stations in the UK, so there's always one nearby. You can recognize them by the MOT sign of three white triangles against a blue background. Not all of them test diesel cars, so if you've got one you'll need to check that out. Some of these stations just do MOT testing but most are linked to garages that will then offer to carry out any repairs.

Testing times

The MOT test can be a nail-biting time for many girls – will your car sail through or will it need lots of expensive repairs? And, as mentioned in Chapter 5, 'The Girls' Guide to Garages', if a garage is going to rip you off, this is an ideal opportunity for them to do it.

Hopefully, by the time your MOT comes round you'll have found a garage you can trust.

But if you haven't, it's worth knowing that many people swear by using council-run MOT centres as a way of keeping costs down. These centres just do MOTs and don't undertake repairs – therefore there's no financial incentive for them to find any faults. You'll find details of your nearest centre on your local authority website.

How much will the MOT cost?

At April 2009 the charge for a car MOT test stands at £53.10. Many garages offer cheaper MOTs, but don't allow yourself to be too influenced by those. If they offer a test more cheaply but are the sort of garage that will 'create' an extra £100 of work out of it, then you haven't got a bargain. Far better to stick with a garage you can trust.

Preparing for the MOT test

It's a good idea to give your car a once-over before you take it in so you're aware of any problems such as worn windscreen wipers or an under-inflated spare tyre, and can remedy some of them yourself if necessary.

During the test

Testing stations do provide viewing areas for customers who want to observe their car going through the test, and if you'd like to do this then by all means do so – it's another good opportunity to learn more.

Failing the test

If your car fails the test you'll be issued with a 'failure' sheet – officially the Notification of Refusal to Issue an MOT Test Certificate (DF). This will list the faults that require correction.

Repairs and re-test

If the failures are pretty minor (maybe a worn tyre or replacement windscreen wipers needed) then it's pretty straightforward – you just pay for those repairs and have it put in for a re-test which it should then pass. If the vehicle is left with the testing station for repair and re-examination there should be no additional MOT fee.

Many testing stations will also do a free re-test if the car is repaired and re-presented to them within a certain time frame, usually seven days, when a full inspection is once again carried out.

If you want to appeal against the test failure

If you're not happy with the result and don't think it's fair, first discuss it with the tester. If that doesn't get you anywhere, contact VOSA within fourteen days and request an appeal form. You'll be offered a re-test, usually within five working days, and you'll be charged for this test. But if your appeal is upheld this will be refunded.

Passing the test

It's always a relief when your car gets through the test – whether that happens at the first attempt or whether it has to have a second run at it. You'll be given a new MOT certificate, which it's important to file away safely.

However, you might also be given an 'advisory notice' – this is a report from the tester flagging up problems that you should get sorted. It's important to act on this as soon as possible rather than putting it into a drawer and forgetting about it – if you don't and you have an accident it may invalidate your car insurance.

Repairs

There are two ways the need for repairs might come to light. One is during a routine service or the MOT test, the other is as the result of an accident, breakdown or from investigating worrying noises, smells or other disturbing symptoms your car has developed. If it's the latter, it's important to be as specific as possible when outlining the problem to the garage – for example, if it has problems starting in the morning.

Second opinions

If you've got a trusted garage, you might want to take their word for it when they quote you a figure for repairs. But in some circumstances you might want to shop around for a second opinion.

> *Toyota charged me £289 for a major service with brake fluid and coolant change – they rang me up an hour into the service and told me I required new front discs and pads for £297. I didn't have them done because it was too expensive. Instead I took it to my local garage who took a look at it and said they were fine. Because it was brakes I tried another one and they said it was fine too. I didn't find challenging the first garage easy but it was worth it for £297.*
> Penny, 22

Also bear in mind that the specialist fitting centres mentioned in the previous chapter can offer very competitive prices on items like tyres and exhausts.

Mysterious car

One of the most frustrating situations you can find yourself in is when there's something wrong with your car but the garage can't get to the bottom of the problem. Driving your car away having been reassured it's been fixed only to have the problem recur and have to take it back again is seriously annoying.

If you're going to a franchised dealer and your problem isn't fixed at the first attempt, then on your second visit ask to speak to the service manager or workshop foreman directly so you can discuss the situation with them in more detail.

If the problem is ongoing then you're going to have to come to an agreement about how much you pay them for diagnosis – most garages do understand that and won't charge you for more than an hour or two. 'But to be honest, if they haven't found it within two hours it's unlikely that they will,' says David Evans of Which?. 'By that point it's a good idea to get a second opinion.'

To repair or not to repair?

Sometimes the news about what your repairs are going to cost is seriously bad – and you find yourself having to make a horrible decision about whether your car is really worth that sort of money or whether it's time to cut your losses and move on.

'It's important to detach yourself emotionally from the car,' says Vanessa Guyll of the AA. 'If you've got an older car and spending £400 will give you two more years of motoring, then that's great. But if that £400 is followed by more repairs which cost £200 and a few months later more work needs doing, then it starts not to be such a good idea. It's difficult to decide where the exact cut-off point should be – but if the cost of repairs is greater than the car's market value then it's time to say goodbye.'

If your car is still worth a reasonable amount, it could be worth paying to have it patched up a bit and then selling it on. But for some cars it really will be the end of the road – and the scrapyard is your only option.

The great car park in the sky

If it's time for your vehicle to go to the Great Car Park in the Sky then you'll need to get it disposed of safely. Under the EU End of Life Directive (which sounds rather *Logan's Run*) cars now have to be recycled as much as possible and this needs to take place at a licensed scrapyard, or Authorised Treatment Facility as they're called nowadays.

It's possible you'll get payment for your vehicle, so do ask. But either way, you won't have to pay to have it taken off your hands. Between them, the two organizations listed below deal with all makes of car found in the UK. Cartakeback also runs a free collection service in many areas of the UK. When you do the handover it's important to have all the paperwork completed properly and to get a Certificate of Destruction (COD) for your car.

⊙ Autogreen, www.autogreen.org, 0800 542 2022
⊙ Cartakeback, www.cartakeback.com, 0845 257 3233

Chapter 7

Getting Beyond 'I'd Like a Pink One'

The best time to start thinking about your next car is long before you need to buy it. If your old one has given up the ghost and you're lost without a car for work or the school run, you're not in a strong position when it comes to haggling at the showrooms or shopping around for the perfect second-hand deal.

Doing your research well in advance means you've got plenty of time to consider your options, which are many and varied. Remember that knowledge is power. And, far from what many people in the motor trade would have you believe, much of that knowledge isn't especially difficult to acquire. And don't think that being a woman will hold you back either – far from it.

'These days both men and women can feel out of their depth when buying a car,' says Steve Fowler, editor of *What Car?*:

> In the past a lot of men used to do their own maintenance and repairs, but over the last twenty years that's really dropped off, partly because cars are becoming more complex and partly because of the pressures of time and modern life. That means these days the average bloke wouldn't necessarily know any more than the average woman – though he'd probably feel he had to pretend he did. Women can actually make better car buyers because they're more pragmatic. If they're not particularly knowledgeable about cars they'll get stuck in and do the research rather than attempt to bluff their way through and that puts them in a stronger position.

Taking on board the advice in this and the following chapter, 'Gotta New Motor?', will help you become car-savvy and virtually impossible to hoodwink, whether you're haggling with a salesman at an upmarket dealership or looking over a ten-year-old Peugeot that you spotted in an advert in your local newsagent's window.

Doing your research

People

When you're thinking of buying a new car, talk to family, friends, neighbours, colleagues, men you meet at dinner parties or on internet dates, other mums you meet at the school gates and taxi drivers about it and ask their advice. Keeping an open mind at this stage is vital, as they could come up with a suggestion that would be off your usual radar but would work really well for you.

National newspapers

The motoring sections of national newspapers can be good for reviews of new models. However, they do mostly prefer to focus on more glamorous and upmarket motors – except when there's fun to be had by sneering at bargain-basement newcomers like the Perodua Viva. Their advice on consumer issues such as car finance and warranties is often excellent though.

Your local paper

This will probably have a motoring section with advice and new car reviews alongside adverts for local dealers and classified ads for private sales. Scanning these can give you an idea of what's available nearby.

Magazines

Autotrader – this is many people's first port of call when looking for a car – there are regional editions so you don't waste your time looking at vehicles at the other end of the country.

What Car? – an indispensable aid for the savvy car buyer. Unlike *Autotrader*, which feels like something your dad might read, *What Car?* is an attractive glossy that's easy to flick through when you're having your highlights done. It has reviews of both used cars and the latest models, advice on getting the best deal and target prices for a huge range of new cars.

Which Car? – an annual publication, containing the full results of its reliability and customer satisfaction surveys. Another accessible and informative read.

The internet is your friend

Forget Google, Facebook and email flirtations – one of the most worthwhile uses of the internet is as a research tool for tracking down your next car. There are some fantastic sites out there that can give detailed information on every aspect of any new or used car you might want to buy.

Most car websites will also help you track down your next car – you put in what you want, the age, condition, price and how far you're willing to travel and some options and prices will ping up!

The websites of Autotrader (www.autotrader.co.uk) and Parkers (www.parkers.co.uk) are both useful for car reviews and valuations. However, www.whatcar.com beats both hands down for user-friendliness – and it also has a link to www.evecars.com, a women's car website with car reviews and news particularly angled to a female readership. It also offers a 'target price', which is the maximum you should expect to pay for a new car at a dealership – print this out and take it along when you set off to the dealership as it's one of the most useful haggling tools you can lay your hands on.

As well as reviews, the *What Car?* website (www.whatcar.com) will let you know how any new car you buy is likely to depreciate in the future, and the trade-in or private sale price you're likely to get for your current car. For example, if you're looking at buying a 2007 Fiat Panda Hatchback 1.1 Active 5dr, this is what you'll probably pay:

- Dealer – £3905
- Private sale – £3590

And if you're selling, you can:

- Ask the private sale price of £3590
- Use it for a part-exchange when buying a new car and aim for a price of £3275
- Sell it to a dealer direct for £3070

The website also gives tips on what to watch out for when buying particular models – for example with a used Mazda MX 5, it's important to check that the heater element in the rear window still works and that the door and bonnet shut tightly and show an even gap between the panels.

And don't miss out on www.honestjohn.co.uk. If you don't have a dad, uncle, boyfriend or mate of the 'I spent years in the motor trade, me, and you can't pull the wool over my eyes' variety on speed dial to accompany you to garages and private sales then Honest John is probably your next best bet. The site gives over 1200 car reviews – the full story on all the popular models on sale in the UK since 1990. It goes into fantastic detail on used cars, warning you exactly what to check out on particular models. So if, for example, you're considering a Nissan Micra built between 1992 and 2003, you'll know that it's vital that the oil has been changed at least every six months, especially if the car has done a low mileage. You'll know that Vauxhall Corsas B (1993–2000) need their coolant levels checked particularly regularly and that you should check the front carpets for signs of damp, which will indicate a failed heater matrix. And that it's important never to buy a second-hand Audi TT Roadster with the top down. Put it up and down a few times to make sure it works properly!

Practicality, passion and price

When buying a car it's important to consider the 3 Ps – practicality, passion and price. The final one tends to be the limiting factor for most people. You might feel that you passionately want a Ferrari, for example, but the price is somewhat off-putting. Or you would ideally like a brand-new people carrier but you're going to have to make do with a second-hand one, complete with the stains where a previous family have spilt chocolate milk in the back.

But with a bit of research and some lateral thinking it can actually be possible to get a lot more 'car for your money' than you might imagine. It is important to think the different issues through carefully first, though – here's a checklist to get you started:

Practicality – what do I need?

New, nearly new, middle-aged or old banger?

Some people see buying a new or newish car as a priority – they like driving a gleaming motor that hasn't been bashed about by previous owners and value having a decent warranty. They tend to change cars every few years, trading their old model in for a newer one.

At the other end of the spectrum are the fans of 'bangernomics' – drivers who either can't or don't want to spend too much on their car and will pick up a cheap car and run it into the ground. If it needs minor repairs they'll get them done but if it develops a major fault they'll cut their losses, pack it off to the scrapyard and start again. If you're interested in learning more about how to make this approach work as cost-effectively as possible check out www.bangernomics.com.

Most people bumble along somewhere in between – the two major influences on their decision-making process being how much money they've got, and positive or painful experiences they've had in the past.

I spent £10,000 – far more money than I could really afford – on an 18-month-old car. I thought it was an investment and that I was buying long-term reliability. What a joke! From a month after the warranty ran out it had one problem after another. I spent a fortune on repairs because I couldn't accept that my 'investment' wasn't working out. In the end I had to sell it off at a loss. Never again will I tie up so much money in a car. It's old bangers for me all the way now – at least if they pack up you haven't lost that much. Katie, 32

I was really lucky in that my parents bought me a brand-new car when I graduated – that was over twenty years ago and I've had new cars ever since. Once you've gone in at that 'higher' level it's relatively easy to stay at it – I just trade my car in as the manufacturer's warranty is about to run out and get another new one. It means that I'm always driving a smart, safe car and I can get most repairs sorted out by the dealership. Lydia, 44

Depreciation

The popular view on buying a new car is that brand-new ones are a poor buy as 'they lose thousands of pounds in value the minute you drive them off the forecourt' – and broadly speaking, that's true. This is down to depreciation (loss of resale value). Cars do depreciate sharply in their early years – and some depreciate more quickly than others. The ones that are good at holding their value are in-demand and classic cars – such as the Mini.

To give a few examples of depreciation:

Kia Picanto Hatchback
New – £5995
Year 1 – £3724
Year 2 – £2778
Year 3 – £2256
Year 4 – £1736

VW Golf Hatchback 1.4
New – £12,235
Year 1 – £8445
Year 2 – £6842
Year 3 –£5758
Year 4 – £4751

Mini Cooper Convertible 1.6
New – £14,960
Year 1 – £11,427
Year 2 – £10,140
Year 3 – £8770
Year 4 – £7685

As you can see, the Mini Cooper still retains half its value after 4 years – while the other two cars drop far more swiftly.

The depreciation index calculator on www.whatcar.com allows you to compare up to four different cars and displays the results in a useful graph – with most cars you'll see a steep drop in the first year, and then more gradual ones thereafter. Incidentally, people in the motor trade often refer to depreciation as 'residuals' – a car having 'good residuals' or 'cast-iron residuals' means it doesn't depreciate quickly.

Different shades of new

If you might be interested in a new or newish car, it's worth bearing in mind that there are different levels of newness.

- **New new** – totally new and ordered from a dealer – this means you can personalize it and order the particular colour and extras you want – and you get that 'new car' smell, of course!
- **Pre-registered new** – this is when a car has been

registered with the DVLA by the dealer. You won't be able to choose the colour or the specification and your name won't be first on the list of owners (the dealer's will) but it is essentially a new car and lots of buyers feel that this makes a good purchase as they're usually about £1000 cheaper than a totally new model.

⊖ **Nearly new** – the definition's unregulated in the UK but it shouldn't be over a year old or have done more than 30,000 miles. It'll be significantly cheaper than a new car.

⊖ **Demo models and management cars** – these are cars that have been used as demonstration and staff cars at a dealership and can make good buys.

Basic new car or classier car second-hand?

As new cars become cheaper, buyers with, say, £6000 can find they can make a choice between a brand-new basic car or a used version of a more upmarket make.

Looking at the example above, you could get a new Kia Picanto at £5995 – which you'd be haggling down to the *What Car?* target price of £5585 (£410 reduction from the list price) and have £415 change out of your £6000. Alternatively you could buy a three-year-old VW Golf for £5758 and have £242 left over.

The Golf is a classier car and better to drive – but then, with the new Kia you'll be getting the three-year manufacturer's warranty and three years without an MOT. It can be an interesting dilemma!

'There are some good deals on new cars out there at the moment,' says Steve Haley of *What Car?*. 'Nearly new can be a few thousands of pounds cheaper than a brand-new car. But then when you factor in the discount you'll be able to get, low-rate finance, and maybe a year's free insurance (which will be more significant if you're a younger driver than an older one) then the gap starts narrowing. It's certainly worth considering for some buyers.'

Manual or automatic?

If you've only got an automatic licence it's not legal for you to drive a manual car without first passing your manual test. If you've got a manual licence then you're qualified to drive both manual and automatic cars. The manual vs automatic debate is an ongoing one. Some drivers really dislike automatics and don't feel they've got the same level of control as they would in a manual. But automatic fans enthuse about the fact that you don't have to fiddle about changing gears the whole time – which can be especially nice in stop-start city traffic. If an automatic appeals then it's worth giving one a test drive and seeing if it suits you. But do bear in mind that manual cars tend to be cheaper to buy and easier to sell on afterwards.

Petrol or diesel?

The petrol vs diesel debate used to go like this – diesel cars hold their value better and can do more m.p.g., so if you do a high mileage then diesel can be better – if not, then go for petrol. However, in the early part of 2008 diesel prices rocketed and the goalposts as regards the mileage level at which diesel is a good buy have shifted dramatically. Before making this particular decision it's important to do the maths based on current and anticipated fuel prices and your own likely mileage.

Size

Do you need a small car that will be great for nipping round town and easy to park? Or a large one to fit your family and friends into? Do you play in a rock band and need to haul your drum kit around? It's important to think this stuff through – and when you get to the point where you're actually going to test-drive the car it can be a good idea to take your children and/or drum kit along to check it really will fit in. And remember, it isn't just the size of the vehicle that's important, but also how flexibly that space can be used.

We chose a Ford Galaxy – it's a seven-seater but five of the seats will fold down flat to the floor, leaving a large boot. With some of the other MPVs we looked at you have to take the seats in and out. Jennifer, 31

Engine size

A small engine size of say 1.1 or 1.2 litres is fine for city driving – though many motorists do like to have rather more power even then. On the motorway, engine sizes of 1.8 and upwards will make driving and overtaking at high speeds easier. Engine size is also linked to the size of the car – small cars can be quite happy with a small engine, whereas MPVs and 4x4s need larger engines – again, upwards of 1.8, with the Volkswagen Touareg having either a 3.6 petrol engine or a 2.5 to 5.0 diesel engine, and the Land Rover Discovery 4.0 petrol or 2.5 diesel. Sports cars also have larger engines – for example with a Mercedes-Benz SLK the petrol engine sizes range between 1.8 and 5.4.

Number of doors

Hatchbacks and estate cars are often referred to as 'three doors' or 'five doors' because the back hatch opening gets counted as a door. Choosing a five-door over a three-door can be a few hundred pounds more expensive, but if you've got children then reaching round to strap them into their car seats can be really tricky without access through the rear doors. But if you only use the back seats when you're giving your mates a lift, then it's not the end of the world if they have to do a bit of clambering in and out.

What sort of journey?

If you're just planning on using the car as a local runaround, things like engine size and whether it's comfortable to drive won't be such a major issue. But if you do regular long journeys then a comfortable car with a large engine will make them easier. And of course if you regularly drive off-road then you'll probably need a 4x4 – but it's not a good idea to get one for your local school run unless you want everyone to hate you.

Reliability

Reliability is high up on everyone's wish list for their ideal car. Here's a run-down on the factors that influence reliability.

The make of car

Some makes of car have got a better reputation for reliability than others. The consumer organization Which? produces an annual *Which? Car Survey* that reports on more than 90,000 cars and shows which makers are consistently reliable. In 2008 the most reliable brands were:

1. Honda
2. Toyota
3. Daihatsu
4. Lexus
5. Mazda

However, it's important to bear in mind that different models within that make can have variable standards – for example, although Honda was top of the reliable brands overall in the Which? survey, the Honda Civic 2006 model came bottom in its medium cars section – so make sure you investigate any car you might buy thoroughly.

And the least reliable (with the worst-performing listed first) were:

1. Chrysler/DodgeRenault
2. Land Rover
3. Renault
4. Fiat
5. Rover

Mileage/age

The higher mileage and the older the car the less reliable they become. But some makes and models of cars cope better with high mileages than others, and diesel cars in particular can go for long distances without too many problems. A high motorway cruising mileage can often be kinder on a car's inner workings than the stop-start of town driving. Check out www.whatcar.com and www.honestjohn.co.uk for the full low-down on any car you might be thinking of buying.

Has it been looked after properly?

Whether the car has been properly looked after in the past is going to influence how it performs in the future. If you're buying a used car it's important to check it's had regular services and any necessary parts replaced at the right time. The www.honestjohn.co.uk website is particularly useful for guidelines about what should have been done (and what might soon need doing) for particular makes and models of cars at particular stages in their life.

Previous owners

It's not just about the mileage the car has clocked up – how it's been driven will also influence the level of wear and tear and how reliable it will be in the future. It's worth doing a spot of detective work to find out more about the previous owner of the car and how they might have treated it.

The boy racer

Mention of 'modifications' such as big exhaust pipes or tinted windows in the advert flag up previous boy-racer ownership. It's likely that this poor car has a long and inglorious track record of handbrake turns and being revved aggressively at traffic lights. Unless you fancy cruising round town with your homies and the boom-box going full blast, this would be a good one to avoid.

The careful lady owner

Ah, this lady is the holy grail of car owners – when she places an advert the phone will start ringing off the hook with people eager to avail themselves of her cast-offs. And her five-year-old Nissan Micra can indeed be a sound investment. However, it's a good idea to ask her what sort of journeys she did in it – although a lifetime of short supermarket runs sounds ideal, the lack of longer drives can cause problems with the battery and oil. It's important that a car that's been driven in this way has also had suitable servicing.

Fleet cars

Fleet cars are ones which have been owned or under contract to a business. Usually they'll have spent most of their life thrashing up and down the motorway with a stressed-out salesperson at the wheel. The mileage tends to be quite high but most will have been properly serviced and at the right price they can be quite a good buy. Make sure you investigate thoroughly when considering an ex-fleet car, however – some dealers try to pass off ex-hire or ex-driving instruction cars as 'fleet cars' and believe me, you don't want to touch either of those options with a ten-foot pole.

Ex-demo models

These are the cars which dealerships use for test drives. The mileage will be low, and they'll usually have been driven respectfully. They can be a very good option.

Safety

Safety is a priority for many of us – particularly those with children. Newer cars are generally safer than older ones – something to bear in mind if you're drawn to going in at the cheaper end of the market. It's a good idea to check out a potential purchase for its NCAP (New Car Assessment Programme) performance – this is an independent test programme where cars are rated for both passenger and pedestrian safety. Incidentally, as far as pedestrian safety goes, bull bars on cars are a really bad idea. They don't provide any protection at all for passengers, and pedestrians hit by a vehicle with them are far more likely to be seriously injured.

Make of car

People often have loyalties towards a certain make of car. It's a bit like families where they always have the same breed of dog – their much-loved Labrador or Collie passes on and after a respectful interval is replaced by another.

I'm mad about Vauxhalls myself. I had a Peugeot once but it had lots of mechanical faults. The clutch cable went once, which I recall being a nightmare to sort out. Anjali, 28

BMW, every time. Very reliable and one of the best at holding their value. Martina, 30

Sometimes this is a good thing – after all, if you're happy with the status quo, why bother to alter it? But when the time to change your car comes around it is worth at least considering other options. Car manufacturers are changing all the time – Skodas used to be a bit of a joke, for example, but now they're very well regarded. So flick through a few car magazines and maybe even test-drive a couple of cars you might not normally have considered. It's a bit like dating men who aren't your usual type or trying on clothes in a colour you wouldn't normally wear – sometimes you can be very pleasantly surprised!

Extras

If you're buying a new car, certain things will be fitted 'as standard' – for example, power steering and driver airbag are both pretty standard these days. Other options such as air conditioning or Bluetooth connection come as 'extras' and will cost more. Clearly this is an area where practicality and passion, needs and wants can overlap. You'll have to decide if you 'need' an MP3/iPod connection because you drive long distances and having your favourite music on tap makes the time go so much faster, or whether you just want one. Obviously the deciding factor will be how much money you have to spend! It's a good idea to look at the different extras and decide which ones matter to you before going to the dealership – that way you don't run the risk of a pushy salesman talking you into unnecessary ones.

It's also important to have an idea of how much each of them costs. As part of the haggling process salespeople often use extras as a bargaining chip – the 'if you buy at this price we'll throw in free metallic paint' strategy. Knowing what that actually adds up to in cold hard cash means you'll know whether to be (secretly) thrilled or unimpressed by their offer.

To give you a rough idea of the sort of prices you might expect to pay for extras in a modern hatchback:

The Renault Twingo Extreme has a list price of £7500.
Power steering, airbags, central locking, CD player and anti-lock brakes are all fitted as standard.

But if you want the following the list prices are:

alloy wheels £500
metallic paint £360
air conditioning £525
climate control £800
MP3/iPod connection £175

Another issue to bear in mind about extras is that some of them 'hold their value' – that is, will help the car get a better price when you come to sell it – and others don't. Air conditioning, for example, is seen as a good investment. But certain extras, such as an interior trim you've ordered to your particular taste, might not necessarily appeal to other people and won't add to the value of the car.

There's also a difference between 'factory fit' extras – i.e. those that are done at the factory, like air conditioning and the paint colour and 'dealer fit' ones which can be installed in the workshop, like mudflaps and towbars. The dealer is more likely to throw in the latter for free as they're easier for him to arrange.

It's just your colour!

If you've always longed for a turquoise or bright pink car then that's great. But before you commit yourself to buying your heart's desire, be aware that it might be more difficult to sell on later. Silver, blue and red are all 'safe' colours when it comes to resale value whereas quirkier ones get fewer potential buyers coming forward. But if you plan to keep your car for more than five years then depreciation becomes less of an issue, and if you want lime-green or purple then you can go for it!

Passion – what do I want?

For some people, a car is just a metal box to carry them around. They want it to be safe, reliable, the right size and, um, that's it. They value substance over style and don't see their car as an extension of themselves in any way.

> *I just can't understand the concept of expressing your personality through your car. I express my personality through what I do and say, and to some extent my clothes and hairstyle and how I decorate my home. But the thought of someone judging me by what sort of car I drive seems as ridiculous as being judged by what make of toaster I've got.* Julia, 55

Certain elements of the motoring press (I'm thinking Jeremy Clarkson here) tend to be rather disparaging about cars that are reliable and economical but lacking in character. 'They're like white goods' or 'They're not fun' are among the kinder descriptions. But frankly, so what? But the thing about fun is that it's a very flexible commodity and people can have it in many different ways – dancing in nightclubs, buying clothes, learning conversational Italian and taking their children to the seaside, to name only a few.

So if buying a cheap, hassle-free car means more money left over for family outings, retail therapy and hobbies that actually mean something to you, then the overall amount of fun in your life is going to be increased rather than decreased by buying a characterless workhorse and you should make that decision with your head held high!

But many of us do harbour yearnings for a car with a certain image and capabilities and that's cool too. This whole process isn't a judgement call, it's just about being honest with yourself as regards your priorities.

Maybe you want a car that says 'I'm fast, sexy and glamorous' such as a Porsche or a Ferrari. Or a VW camper van that you can take to Glastonbury Festival or use to camp out at the beach in true hippie-chick style.

If you're passionate about wanting a particular car then it's worth putting your thinking cap on and working out how you can get it. For example, everyone knows that sports cars are expensive – but many makes depreciate fast and you can often pick up an older one at a bargain price. Or you could substitute a cheaper model for the one you originally had in mind – for example, a new Ferrari will set you back at least £129,000, and a Porsche about £34,000 – but you can get a used Mazda MX5 for about £3000 and still get that fun, sporty driving experience.

But sometimes it isn't just the price that holds wannabe flash motor owners back.

I always wanted a two-seater sports car but felt I couldn't have one because it would mean that I couldn't give a lift to more than one of my friends at the same time. But then I realized I hardly ever did that anyway. And even if I couldn't, it wasn't like it would be the end of the world – they could travel with other friends or get a cab or something. It wasn't a valid reason to deny myself my dream car. Elinor, 27

In the case of VW camper vans it's not so much the cost as the maintenance problems which can deter potential buyers –

the early split-screen and bay-window models are as adorably vintage as you could ever wish for, but they are martyrs to rust and you'll be doomed to ongoing work to keep it at bay. However, if you buy one of the later models, say a Type 3 onwards, then although it won't look as stylish it won't saddle you with heartbreaking repair bills either.

So when it comes to motoring passions, it's a case of checks and balances and working out what's really important to you. And even if you can't afford what you want right now, maybe you can buy a car which at least gives you a taste of your ideal. For example, you might not be able to buy a convertible, but maybe you could get a car with a sunroof to give you that summery fresh-air feeling? Or if you've got hordes of children and an MPV is your best option, but the thought of driving something so uncompromisingly sensible makes your heart sink, then perhaps you could still go for one that's got reasonably stylish design values, such as the Citroën C4 Picasso MPV.

Price – how much am I prepared to pay?

When it comes to budgeting for your car, there are three factors you need to take into consideration.

How much you pay for it
This is just the basic price if you're paying cash, or the basic price plus the cost of the interest payments if you're buying it with a loan or other finance agreement.

How much it's going to cost you to run
This covers road tax, insurance, fuel, servicing, breakdown and repair costs. Check out Chapter 2, 'Money and Your Motor', Chapter 5, 'The Girls' Guide to Garages', and Chapter 9, 'Car

Insurance Uncovered', for a rough idea of what you might be paying and then do detailed research on the costs for the car you've got in mind before going ahead.

Depreciation

This is an important factor and one covered in detail in the 'Depreciation' section above on buying a new or newish car (p. 131).

It's important to think very clearly about how much you're willing to spend on your car and how that's going to fit in with the rest of your budget. It'll help you be firm about what you do or don't want before you look at your first used car ad in the newspaper or walk into a dealership. That way you won't end up letting a dealer coax you into extras you don't really need then get home and realize you can't afford a holiday or to turn your central heating on.

Chapter 8

Gotta New
Motor?

So you've decided what sort of car you want and how much you're willing to pay. Which means the time has now come to actually track down your heart's desire and buy it. Unfortunately this is a process that can be full of pitfalls for the unwary. But the more prepared you are the better able you'll be to avoid them and to come away with a fantastic car at a bargain price. Here are some basic principles to bear in mind.

Take it slowly

Sometimes it's fun to buy things on impulse. A book, a bunch of flowers or a pair of shoes can all provide a delightful, life-enhancing fillip of retail therapy. Cars, however, don't fit into this category and it's vital not to rush into buying the first one that takes your fancy.

You might be flicking through a magazine when you spot a stylish city car advertised with an enticingly low interest rate and modest monthly repayments. How tempting to just fling the mag aside and dash off to the nearest dealership for a test drive! But before you do, check whether the interest quoted is APR or a flat rate. The difference could run into hundreds or even thousands of pounds.

Or, at the other end of the scale, maybe your neighbour is offering his old car at a knockdown price – what a result! But if it's got a powerful engine and you're a newly qualified driver the insurance costs are likely to be high. It's essential to get an insurance quote before taking things any further.

Remember, this is a time when it's cool to be cautious. Don't go making a snap decision that you'll end up regretting every time you open your bank statement for the next five years.

Is it different for girls?

As Steve Haley, editor of *What Car?*, pointed out in the previous chapter, women can empower themselves by thoroughly researching their options and having all the facts and figures at their fingertips before they go anywhere near a dealer fore-court. However, it would be unrealistic to pretend that the old assumptions and prejudices about women and cars don't exist and there's a reasonable chance that you'll come up against them at some point.

> *My husband and I recently bought a new car and I found the salesmen in some garages would almost seem to use my husband as an interpreter when replying to my questions. The conversation would go something like this:*
> *Me: how many owners has this car had and does it have a full service history?*
> *Salesman (to my husband): It's had two owners and has an FSH.*
> *Me: The clutch seems to be slipping a bit, would you repair this if we buy the car?*
> *Salesman (to my husband): Yes, we would.*
> *Me (to my husband): I'm not sure, let's go and look elsewhere.*
> Martina, 30

This sort of behaviour is tedious and the best way to respond to it is to take your custom elsewhere. After all, if a dealer is ignoring or patronizing you at the point at which they're meant to be trying to win your custom, it doesn't bode well for the sort of treatment you're likely to get if you need after-sales service such as repairs.

By the same token, try to get a feel for the person you'll be dealing with if you're calling up about a private sale – if they treat your questions about issues such as the car's condition or history in an offhand manner, then ask yourself if this is really someone you want to do business with. Always remember that as the buyer you're in a strong position and that there's absolutely no reason to spend any of your time or money with someone who doesn't treat you with respect.

It's a small print world

Do you enjoy reading small print? Comparing interest rates, analysing warranty exclusion clauses and checking service history records? You don't? Oh, that's a pity! Because if you're buying a car (especially a new or newish one) you're going to be doing rather a lot of it. And it's really important that you don't skimp on it. When buying a car, people tend to focus their concerns on mechanical matters and worry about head gaskets going, durability of crankshafts and so on. But, frankly, these days you're just as likely to lose money through getting stitched up by misleading paperwork as buying a crock.

If you're buying your car through a dealer, one of the main print-fests you're likely to be confronted with is your car warranty. So before we go any further, here are some guidelines to what's hot and what's not in the world of car warranties.

Your car warranty

It's a guarantee, but not as we know it

Car warranties are similar to the guarantee you'd get with your kettle, only loads more complicated. If you buy a kettle and it's guaranteed for a year you know exactly where you stand. If anything goes wrong you can get it replaced or repaired.

Car warranties, on the other hand, are full of small print. If they were made for kettles they'd say things like, 'Well, we'll repair the heating element, but if anything goes wrong with the plug you'll have to pay for that yourself. And you'll have to bring the kettle in every six months to have it serviced at our shop, which will cost you 50p each time. Oh, and if you boil it more than 10 times a day then the warranty will be declared invalid.'

Now, I'm not telling you this to put you off warranties. A good warranty can offer you a certain peace of mind – the knowledge that as long as you comply with the conditions, the cost of certain repairs that might come up while you've got it will be covered.

It's just to let you know that even decent warranties are complicated things – they've got inclusion clauses, exclusion clauses and can be rendered invalid by things like not having your car serviced at particular intervals or driving it more than a certain number of miles a year. And poor warranties are a complete waste of your money, as they've got so many exclusion clauses that they can wriggle out of paying for most things.

They invariably have a clause that excludes failure due to 'wear and tear', which pretty much cuts out anything that is ever likely to fail! I only discovered this when I needed a new clutch for my car and then the sunroof started leaking. I got in touch with the warranty company only to find that neither was covered because of the 'wear and tear' issue.
Rochelle, 25

Here's a rundown of the various warranties available – from the lengthy ones you get with brand-new cars right through to the three-month variety you might be offered by a second-hand dealer when you buy a 12-year-old Vauxhall Astra.

What they've all got in common is that they need to be studied with great care. Knowing the exact terms of your car warranty, or a personal warranty you might potentially sign up for, is essential. Read it when you're in a narrow-eyed, suspicious frame of mind (and if you're of a sunny and trusting disposition then get a habitually sour-faced friend or relative to go over it with you).

Manufacturers' warranties

One of the most appealing things about a new car for many motorists is that it will come with a manufacturer's warranty – these tend to be more comprehensive than those offered by car dealers or many independent warranty providers.

How long will the warranty last?

Three years has become fairly standard, though Hyundai have recently introduced a five-year warranty. Longer warranties can push up the resale value of a car as you can run it for three years and sell it with two years of the manufacturer's warranty still intact.

So, this means I don't get any repair bills for at least the first three years, right?

Er, not exactly. When you read the small print in your warranty you'll see that it doesn't cover 'non-warranty items'. These are generally what's described as 'frictional parts' which are meant to wear out in the normal course of events, such as tyres, windscreen wipers, clutches and brakes. If anything goes wrong with these you'll be expected to pay out for parts and labour yourself.

However, if a part is meant to last for, say, ten years, but breaks down after two, the manufacturer may make a 'goodwill payment' towards the cost of repairing it – this is at their discretion, however.

What do I have to do to keep the warranty valid?
You'll have to have it serviced to the standards and at the frequency laid down by the manufacturer. If you use a franchised garage for this, it can be expensive. Going to an independent garage will probably be cheaper, but it's important to ensure that it's one which will use the parts and procedures stipulated by the manufacturer – this issue is discussed in detail in Chapter 6, 'Services, MOTs and Repairs'. Missed and late services are one of the main reasons that warranty claims are turned down, so it's really important to stay on top of them.

Your warranty might also set down a maximum mileage – say 60,000 miles over three years. If you might do a higher mileage than this then find out what the consequences will be.

Different manufacturers have different reputations for their attitude towards dealing with warranty repairs. Toyota, Hyundai and Honda have good records for getting stuck in without quibbling, while certain others have a tendency to try to get out of it.

Ooh, I get free breakdown cover!
Many new car warranties offer free breakdown cover – but this is often only for the first year. If yours runs out after that you'll have to make other arrangements.

Body and paint cover – don't miss out!
Some warranties include body and paint cover and the period covered can be quite lengthy – up to as long as thirty years.

However, there's generally a clause in the warranty saying that you have to have your car inspected every year to keep these items valid. Don't rely on your dealer to remind you about this because they often forget. This part of the warranty can be transferred to future owners, so keeping it valid can help with the resale value of your car.

Extended warranties (sometimes called after-market or personal warranties)

When the new-car warranty has run out, it's possible to buy an extended warranty. You'll probably be offered one by your dealer, but you'll generally get a better deal by going directly to a warranty company. It's important to shop around as the level of coverage and the price you pay can vary dramatically.

You might also be interested in getting an extended warranty for a used car you've bought – you can call up a warranty company, give them details of your car and get a provisional quote. They normally only warranty cars under ten years old and a typical quote might be in the region of £300 a year.

Pre-warranty inspection requirement and cost

Some warranty companies will want to check out your car before they offer to provide any sort of guarantee for it. It's understandable that they don't want to take on a car that's totally knackered, but these inspections can take up to two hours and leave you with a bill of about £150 – and that's even before you've paid for the policy.

Maximum claim limit

Some companies have quite a low ceiling for the maximum amount you can claim, meaning you've got to shell out for the extra costs yourself – this is a really important one to check out.

Mileage and servicing requirements
As with new car warranties, extended ones often require that your car is serviced regularly and states a mileage you mustn't exceed.

Inclusion and exclusion cover
Exclusion warranties are easier to understand as they only list the items which aren't covered. Inclusion warranties list the parts covered in the policy document. It'll probably be a long and seemingly comprehensive list but it's important to check it carefully as some quite important items such as catalytic converters might be left off.

Consequential loss cover
This is when something that isn't covered by the warranty (say, the cam-belt) goes, and wrecks bits of the engine that are covered. Will the company still shell out for the covered bits or not? Going through the consequential loss section with a fine-tooth comb will tell you. It will also probably be one of the most tedious things you ever do in your life, but worth it if you want to avoid shelling out for a policy that's going to let you down when you need it most.

Wear and tear
In particular, look out for the dreaded 'wear and tear' exclusion clause. As the name suggests, it means the warranty doesn't cover damage and breakdowns which come about as a result of 'wear and tear'. This is a seriously limiting factor, as most things that could ever go wrong can probably be interpreted as the result of 'wear and tear'.

Some people think it's better to put the money you'd pay out for a premium into a savings account and then draw on it directly if you need repairs in the future. That can be a good strategy, but it can be worth at least investigating the extended warranty option as well.

If you do decide to go down the personal warranty route, Warranty Direct – www.warrantydirect.co.uk, 0800 731 7001 – has got a decent reputation. Unlike many companies it does pay out for 'wear and tear' and for 'consequential loss' problems and faults discovered during services and MOTs. Their cover includes shock absorbers, drive shaft, the gearbox and engine and all garage labour costs.

Used-car warranties for 'newish' cars

If you're buying a newish car, it's likely that some of the original three-year warranty will still be left to run. It's especially important, however, to check that the previous owner kept to any servicing or mileage requirements – if they didn't, then the warranty will be invalid.

If you're buying a newish car from a dealer they'll probably offer a one-year warranty – but it can get confusing if there's still some of the original manufacturer's warranty still to run. It sort of works along the lines of:

> If it's a one-year-old car with two years of the new car warranty still to run you'll get that.
>
> If it's two and a half years old you get the remaining six months of the new car warranty and six months of a used-car one (usually less comprehensive).
>
> If it's three years old then you'll get a one-year used-car warranty.

Used-car warranties for older cars

If you're buying an older car from a second-hand car dealer, they'll generally offer a warranty of about three months – what it covers in terms of parts and labour can vary considerably, so check it out carefully.

Post-warranty claims

One of the cruel tricks that life sometimes likes to play is that your car will suffer some major mechanical catastrophe about one week after the warranty runs out. Some manufacturers will allow you to put in a 'post-warranty claim' and contribute towards the cost of repairs – but this is very much at their discretion.

If you're not happy with how a warranty claim has been handled

Contact your local Citizens Advice Bureau, or use the Which? Legal Service mentioned in Chapter 5, 'The Girls' Guide to Garages' (p. 107).

What about my old car?

It's important to think about what you're going to do with your old car before you enter into buying a new one. The options are:

- ☉ Trading it in with the dealer you're buying your new car from – he may then go on to spruce it up a bit and sell it on his forecourt or send it off to be sold at auction.
- ☉ Selling it privately – you can sell your car through advertising in the local paper, or a magazine like *Autotrader*, advertising it on an internet site such as eBay or letting family, friends and colleagues know you've got a car for sale.

Which to choose?

You can get significantly more selling your car privately than by trading it in. But with private sales you've also got all the palaver of advertising it, having people come to your home to look it over, making sure they're insured for test drives, sorting out the paperwork and the payment handover and so on.

The option you choose is going to be influenced by balancing out how much you want the extra cash vs how unenthusiastic you are about the hassles that come with selling your car privately.

To find out what sort of difference you'll be looking at, check out the different prices on www.whatcar.com – to look back at the prices mentioned for the 2007 Fiat Panda Hatchback in Chapter 7, if you were selling this car privately you could expect £3590, if you sold it as a trade-in, £3275 or directly to a dealer, £3070. So, let's say you're looking at the difference between trading it in or selling it privately – that's £315. And whether £315 is worth it to you is going to depend on how comfortable you are with the process and what your bank statements have been looking like recently.

There are also internet sites, such as www.webuyanycar.com, which will give you an online valuation for your car – but the offers do tend to be at rock-bottom prices so it's best to check out other options first.

Who shall I buy my car from?

Franchised dealership

These will sell new and nearly new cars, all of a particular make such as Mazda or Volvo. This is the most expensive option, but you also get the best levels of warranty cover and legal protection. They'll also provide a range of finance options including loans, hire purchase and probably leasing as well.

Second-hand dealership

This includes everything from large dealerships to garages that just sell a few used cars off their forecourt. You'll generally find a mixture of makes and ages and some dealerships specialize in particular types of cars such as ex-fleet cars or automatics. The dealers will probably get an MOT done before putting it on their forecourt and they'll usually offer a warranty but it'll generally be a shorter and less comprehensive warranty than you'd be offered at a franchised dealership. Some of these warranties are backed by a third party rather than the dealer, so that if they go out of business you'll still have someone to turn to.

Both franchised and second-hand dealerships will probably be able to take your old car as a trade-in. Another advantage of going to a dealership is that they'll be familiar with the paperwork issues and be able to guide you through them.

However, one of the main incentives for using a dealer is that they've got to comply with the Sale of Goods Act and sell goods that are 'of satisfactory quality and free from defects unless they are brought to your attention by him' – and this does give you a degree of legal protection.

It's good to use a dealership that's a member of one of the trade associations, such as the Society of Motor Manufacturers and Traders (SMMT): www.smmt.co.uk, 020 7235 7000; the Retail Motor Industry Federation (RMIF): www.rmif.co.uk, 020 7580 9122; or the Scottish Motor Trade Association: www.smta.co.uk, 0131 331 5510.

Car supermarket

Car supermarkets have rather a mixed reputation. The profit margins are low and they work on a 'pile 'em high and sell 'em cheap' approach – there certainly isn't much room for haggling and many salespeople here will refuse to do it. Test drives will be brief – and some car supermarkets don't offer them at all. With car supermarkets it's important to bear in mind that they make much of their profit not from the car itself but from getting you to take out a high-interest loan to pay for the car, selling insurance, payment protection and extended warranties and so on. If you're confident, then by all means check out what's on offer at your local car supermarket – and even buy if the price is right. But it's wise to be cautious when it comes to their loans and insurance deals.

Buy through a private sale

You can get some real bargains this way, but it's also the most time-consuming, what with having to . . . (deep breath . . .) go through the local paper and call up about cars that have already gone and then finally find one that hasn't and sort out insurance so you can take a test drive and trail out to their house on a Saturday afternoon when you'd rather be shopping or playing baseball in the park and poke about their old Renault Clio, and then try to sort out HPI checks and maybe an AA or RAC one too and then make all sorts of complicated arrangements for handing the money over – and at the end of it drive away knowing that you don't have much legal protection if the car falls apart tomorrow . . .

So yes, buying through a private sale can be an economical choice but certainly has its pitfalls. The only legal protection you've got is that the car must be 'as described' – so that's why it's important to keep the advert and any supporting documents afterwards. And of course cadging a car loan from Mrs Jones of Acacia Avenue isn't going to be an option so if you don't have the ready cash you'll need to have taken out a loan in advance and have the money in your current account and ready to go.

Private sales through family, friends and neighbours

This can work well as there'll be more trust there on both sides. However, there can be drawbacks – such as if the car develops serious problems a few months later and, of course, the issue of how much you're going to pay.

I bought my last car off a friend which was easy and hassle-free, but a bit awkward when it came to negotiating a price. Nuala, 33

Buying at auction

You can get a real bargain at a car auction – or end up with a total crock! The cars available are generally a mixture of ex-fleet cars, cars that have been repossessed and those used as trade-ins at dealerships. They might have a form attached to the windscreen giving details of their history, but many are 'sold as seen' and you just have to take your chances.

The auction will move very quickly and you don't get much of a chance to look over the car during the actual auction though with some you can turn up early and check cars over then. Most auction houses won't allow you to take a test drive.

If you're thinking of buying at auction then go along to a couple just to check them out first. You'll find details of local car auction sites in your local Yellow Pages. Most of them have several sales a week, with the daytime ones being mostly people in the car trade and the evening or weekend ones being private buyers.

Auction houses generally have a fee called a 'Buyer's Premium', which you pay to the house in addition to the cost of the car. The rates will be displayed somewhere in the auction hall, so find out how much they are before taking the plunge and bidding. And if you do decide to buy this way, don't get caught up in the heat of the moment and bid way over your limit, whatever you do!

Buying over the internet

Some car sales over the internet are just ordinary private sales that happen to use the net as an advertising medium, such as eBay. Others are actual businesses which sell cars over the net – one of these is www.carsite.co.uk, which sells ex-fleet cars, all of which have been RAC and HPI checked. It's also got a female-friendly sister site at www.galscarguide.co.uk, which is worth checking out.

Brokers, discounters and importers

These companies have commercial relationships with various car sellers and thus set their own prices or source cheaper cars from Europe. The main ones are autofinders, jamjar, drivethedeal, newcar4me and ukcarbroker.

If you're buying from an importer it's important to check everything, including whether it's an EU or non-EU import, the warranty situation, breakdown cover and whether the car is left- or right-hand drive.

Before going down any of these routes it's a good idea to check out the price that you could get through one of the mainstream buying routes and then decide whether the difference is worth it.

The top seven car-buying mistakes and how to avoid them

One – buying a stolen car

About one in 300 cars is registered as stolen and many people have bought one in good faith, only to then get a visit from the police, keen to return it to its rightful owner.

How to avoid it
Many dealers will only sell cars which have been HPI checked (this is a thorough history check looking at whether a particular car has been stolen, clocked or has an outstanding loan against it).

If you're interested in a car which hasn't had this check it's a good idea to have it done independently – contact them via www.hpicheck.com or call 01722 422 422. The current cost of the service is £19.99 and you can get an immediate check online, and a certificate within 48 hours. You can also do these checks via the AA or RAC.

If you're looking at a private sale car and the 'owner' seems confused about some aspect of the car – doesn't know where the bonnet release catch is, for example, then that should set alarm bells ringing. Another classic sign of a stolen car is a lack of accompanying paperwork – the V5, MOT certificates and so on. Don't accept any excuses of the 'it's in the post', 'I've just moved house and it's packed in one of the boxes and I don't know which one', or 'my dog ate it' variety. Just make an excuse of your own and leave.

Two – buying a 'cut and shut', accident-damaged or 'clocked' car

Beware of cars that have been damaged or tampered with – as well as being bad buys, they can be dangerous. An HPI check will help you spot them – but here are a few extra checks you can do.

'Cut and shut' cars

This is where the front half of one written-off car gets joined to the rear half of another. You might imagine that the end result would look rather Frankenstein-ish, but in fact if the welding and respraying is done well they can be almost undetectable to the untrained eye. There are currently about 30,000 cut-and-shut cars in the UK and most people wouldn't recognize one if they saw it. Go through the paperwork carefully and in particular check the VIN number of the vehicle against the V5 registration document.

Watch out for uneven panel gaps or mismatched paint shades on the car. Another giveaway is if the boot needs a different key from the rest of the car.

Accident damage

Even if a car looks structurally sound after an accident, the 'jolt' to all the systems can have a knock-on effect long after the event. Look out for signs of structural damage and ask the owner if it's been in any accidents.

Clocking

This is where the odometer has been fiddled with to give a lower mileage and hence make the car more attractive to buyers. Examine the paperwork properly – the mileage is always recorded on MOT certificates so these should go up in say 8,000 or 10,000 increments – and not go backwards at any point!

The other method is to examine the general appearance of the car – if the seller is claiming it's only done 10,000 miles but the steering wheel, footwell or seats are very worn, it's time to ask yourself, 'what's wrong with this picture?'

Three – buying from a trader pretending to be a private seller

Private sellers aren't responsible for the quality of the car under the Sale of Goods Act in the same way that dealers are. So dodgy dealers will pretend to be private sellers to shirk responsibility. And of course, dealers who are willing to do this are also more likely to do other dodgy stuff like sell vehicles that have been stolen or 'clocked'.

How to avoid it

When you first phone up, say 'I'm calling about the car', then if they say 'What car?' you'll know there are several available and the seller is probably a trader. Traders may well offer to bring the car to you, or suggest you meet at a halfway point like a service station car park – always refuse and insist on coming to their home address.

When you're checking out the V5, make sure it's got the name and address of a private seller, not a dealer as the last owner – and if it hasn't then walk away, no matter how plausible they might seem.

Four – buying a crock

This is a slightly different issue from the three previous ones. With those, you're dealing with someone who is consciously trying to defraud you. If you've got good 'dodgy people' radar you'll probably be able to work out that something doesn't quite add up and back off without even having to bother with HPI reports.

But when it comes to a crock, you'll probably be dealing with someone who's just an ordinary Joe or Joanna. Maybe they're aware that the car is getting a bit knackered and are keen to play 'pass the parcel' so that someone else gets landed with the big bills rather than them. Or maybe the car is doing fine at the moment but is doomed to conk out soon.

And of course it's possible to buy a crock from a second-hand dealer as well as through a private sale. Dealers who value their reputation won't put anything too wrecked on their forecourt, but even the decent ones can make errors of judgement.

How to avoid it

This is actually an area where a degree of mechanical knowledge is going to come in useful. If the car seems promising and you've got any car-savvy people in your family or social circle, this is a good time to call on them and ask them to come along with you to look at it. Or if you've got a good relationship with your local independent garage, it might be worth asking one of the mechanics if you could pay them their usual hourly rate to come with you. Another good strategy is to have the car checked out by AA or RAC mechanics – the AA charge £136 for a basic check and £184 for a longer one. However, it may take a few days to arrange and if a private seller gets a firm offer elsewhere then they'll probably be inclined to accept that rather than hang around for you – this is a time when you'll have to use your powers of persuasion.

As far as doing what checks you can yourself – use reviews on www.honestjohn.co.uk and www.whatcar.com for information about the particular problem areas you should be looking out for. However, some general guidelines include:

- If it's a private-sale car try to place your hand on the bonnet to see if it's been driven and warmed up just before your arrival to hide any problems it might have starting from cold.
- Start the car (while your friend is standing nearby) and they can check the colour and amount of the exhaust smoke. Too much smoke is a bad sign and blue smoke indicates a worn engine.
- Open the bonnet and check for any obvious fluid leakage.
- Check the tyres for signs of excessive wear or damage.
- During the test drive don't talk too much – keep listening out for any unusual noises or vibrations, and keep an eye on the different instrument panels (speedometer, petrol gauge, warning lights) to check that they seem to be working OK.

Five – getting fiddled on the finance

One of the most important things to remember when buying a new or newish car is that dealerships don't just make money out of selling cars – they also make money out of selling finance. That means it's important to examine any loans or purchase agreements carefully to ensure they're the best possible deal for you.

For most girls, taking out a personal loan from a bank or building society will be your best bet. But it's worth checking out what's on offer at the dealership as well – be wary and read the small print though. Here are some things you should especially watch out for.

Flat rate means steeper borrowing costs

Always check whether the interest rate you're being offered is flat rate or APR. Flat-rate interest is really bad news – it means interest is charged on the original amount borrowed, no matter what's been repaid. So if, say, you borrow £5000 at 6 per cent flat-rate interest, you're still paying interest on the whole amount even in the final year when debt has been reduced. Whereas if you borrow under APR, as the debt goes down, so does the interest.

And it's a big difference:

For a loan of £5000 over five years at 6 per cent APR – the cost of borrowing is £800

For a loan of £5000 over five years at 6 per cent flat rate – the cost of borrowing is £1500

Now you see it, now you don't – 0% finance

Some dealerships will draw your attention to a car by putting '0% finance' in really big type in the advert – but then when you look closer it's only 0% for the first year, then goes up after that. Yet another reason to read the small print!

There are more than four weeks in a month, actually

When talking about how much a particular car will cost you,

dealers often prefer to talk in terms of weeks – 'it's only £57 per week', for example, implying that the repayments are £228 a month, or £2736 per annum. But as there are 52 weeks in a year, it's really 52 x £57 = £2964 per annum. That's £228 a year more! Always multiply the weekly cost to a yearly one to work out what you'll really be paying.

Plastic might not be that fantastic

If you're thinking that you might put your car on a low-rate credit card, be aware that some dealers don't accept them – and that some that do charge a 1 or 2 per cent fee.

Payment protection insurance

When you're taking out any sort of loan, whether that's from a bank or a car dealer they will probably try and talk you into getting PPI (payment protection insurance). The idea is that this will help pay off the loan if you fall ill or are made redundant. However, PPI hasn't got a very good reputation as there tend to be so many get-out clauses for the lender. So if you're offered PPI by your dealer it's best to avoid it.

Incidentally, some really underhand dealers will conveniently 'forget' that you didn't want PPI and when they print out the finance documents it will be included – if you challenge them then they'll just say it was a mistake. Another reason to read any finance documents very slowly and very carefully.

Additional credit charges

Some finance deals look OK . . . but then you notice the additional credit charges. Here's an example – in May 2008 my local dealership is offering a Renault Twingo Extreme for £7777.

The terms of the loan (finance) they're offering are 5.9 per cent APR over 47 months – so at least there's no nasty flat-rate interest there! But in the small print there's also an 'acceptance fee' of £99, and a 'credit facility fee' of £139. This makes the cost of taking out the loan £1121, £883 of which is interest on the loan, £238 of which is these extra charges.

There is one question you must always ask when taking out car finance and it's 'What's the total that I'll repay, including all charges?' And of course, it's always worth trying to get those extra charges knocked off!

Six – falling for the dealer's sales patter

Salespeople at dealerships are trained to sell cars – and some of the strategies they use to do that, such as trying to build up your enthusiasm for the car, are to be expected and it's not really fair to see them as 'tricks'. However, there are other strategies that you need to be aware of so you can avoid being taken in by them.

'I've got the perfect car for you'

If a dealer has had a car sitting on their forecourt that they just can't shift then chances are they're wondering if you're the girl they can offload it onto. By all means look at it if it's within your price range but if it's not the car for you then be firm about that and ask to look at the ones already on your list.

'This would be the ideal car for you – and it's only slightly over your budget'

Dealers will often try to push you to go over the price limit you've set yourself. Be firm and remember that, although the car or the extras they're pushing may well be appealing, they're going to mean cutting back on holidays, clothes or family expenses.

'This offer is only available today'

Take this one with a huge pinch of salt. The thing to remember about buying a car is that the dealer is on their home turf and you're not. That means they've got the opportunity to do the hard sell on finance deals, get pushy about the value of different extras, query the worth of your vehicle as a trade-in and so on. At the showroom you've only got their word to go on – but if you take the information away and check it over either by yourself, with a friend or over the internet then the balance of power is restored, and many dealers aren't keen on that, hence the pressure to make a decision on the spot.

'I can't talk about discounts unless you leave a deposit'

Now that's just being silly. Why would you want to tie up money in a deal when you don't yet know if it's going to be a good one or not?

'I'll have to clear this with my manager'

It's worth being a tad sceptical about this. They might try and play the 'I'd love to give you this deal but my manager won't let me' card – so ask to speak to the manager yourself. Sometimes they'll bring another dealer back and try out the 'good cop, bad cop' routine. Don't let yourself be swayed by it and walk away if necessary.

Seven – what are these extra charges and why are they on my bill?

As well as the extra credit charges mentioned in 'getting fiddled on the finance', there can be additional costs related to buying a car from a dealership – 'delivery charges', 'administration charges' and so on. Ask if there will be any extra costs and what they will relate to before signing any deal.

Buying your car

So you've read the car magazines, surfed the internet car sites, printed out information about the cars you might be interested in — and you're actually ready to go and look at a few and hopefully find one you'll want to buy! This section will guide you through the process, give tips and help you avoid the pitfalls at each stage.

It takes two

It's fine to do the initial reconnaissance by yourself, but when you get to the point of checking over a second-hand car, taking test drives or handing over large amounts of money it's a good idea to take along a friend or relative. Ideally this will be some-one who knows a bit about cars, but if no one you know fits into that category, anyone supportive will do, or a mechanic from your local garage (expect to pay their usual hourly rate).

Get your timing right

Sometimes choosing the right time can help you get the right price.

Dealership

Car dealers have monthly targets to meet and if they haven't done so as the month draws to its close they'll be especially keen to make a sale – and so your chance of getting a good discount is increased. And the ends of the yearly quarters – March, June, September and December – can be even better. Counter-seasonal buying can work well too – for example convertibles can be cheaper in December than June. It's also a good idea to note when a particular model is going to be superseded, as they'll be keen to sell the older models and discounts will be easier.

Private sale

The monthly and quarterly timing issue is more of a dealer than a private-sale thing. With private sales, timing is more about time of day. Viewing a car in the evening is often more convenient when both parties have day jobs – but it's not a good idea to look over a car in the dark as this can hide a lot of defects. In the winter, try to arrange weekend viewings.

The phone call – it's good to talk

A chat over the phone can help make your dealership visit as productive as possible – and help you decide whether a private sale car is even worth bothering about. In both instances ask about the insurance situation – will you be insured to take the car out on a test drive? – if not, you'll need to arrange cover yourself.

Dealership

If you think you might want to take a test drive or two, call up the dealership first to check the model you're interested in is available, and to arrange a suitable time.

Private sale

If you're buying through a private sale and don't want to travel too far check the dialling code in the advert to find out where it is – use www.ukphoneinfo.com. During the call, confirm with the owner that they've got all the relevant documents to hand. Also have a general chat about the car – confirming the details in the advert about how much road tax and MOT it's got left and filling in any gaps that might not have been mentioned in the advert, such as the service history. Make arrangements to meet at their home and don't forget to give them your number and ask them to get in touch if they sell it to someone else beforehand – you don't want to end up making a wasted journey. If you're bringing a friend along then it's only polite to let them know.

Let's get physical – looking at the car

So, it's time to sit in the car, see if it feels comfortable, check that your stuff will fit in and so on. It can feel a bit awkward doing this, as the checks you'll want to make will probably take a while. This is one of the reasons it's so good to have someone else there at this point – they can keep the dealer or seller talking while you poke around (or vice versa, if they're the more mechanically inclined one).

Dealership

Be aware that this is the point at which many dealers will try to steer you towards the more expensive models of car and will also try to play on any feelings you're developing for certain aspects of the car, whether that's the leather interior or safety features. This is a normal part of the sales process and doesn't fit into the 'dodgy dealer' category, but it is important to be aware of it. The dealer might also offer you some coffee, but think twice before accepting. It's usually scalding hot and many people feel obliged to stay and drink it, which means the dealer has you as a 'captive audience'. But at this stage you need to be able to beat a hasty retreat if you realize the car isn't for you.

Private sale

For the same 'quick getaway' reason, ignore any offers of cups of tea or coffee. You'll want to carry out more checks on an old car than you would on a gleaming showroom model – run through the ones outlined in 'buying a crock' (p. 167) and check out the condition of the interior. And take along a tape or CD with you so that you can check the music system works.

The test drive – testing, testing

The test drive is a vital part of the process – a car that seems great, both on paper and in terms of looks, just might not 'feel' right when you get behind the wheel. There are some situations where a test drive might not be possible – they're rare at auction houses, for example, and some internet car-selling sites don't allow them for insurance reasons. As a potential buyer the absence of test-drive facilities would be something you'd just have to factor into the equation and decide whether the other benefits were enough to offset it.

It's important to make sure that you've got all the necessary legal cover before you get into the car – so check that the car has valid road tax and MOT and that you're insured to drive it.

Ideally, do your test drive on a route you're familiar with so that you can concentrate on the car rather than the traffic. Listen for any rattles, bumps or strange noises from the engine, and the extent to which you get wind noise on a motorway or dual carriageway. Also, pay special attention to the steering and how comfortable it feels for you. Ideally you should do at least ten to fifteen miles, though some private sellers might not be keen on your taking that much time. However, if you're going to drive regularly on the motorway then doing a stretch of either that or a dual carriageway is important. And, embarrassing as it might feel, have a go at parking in a really tight spot – if you're going to have problems with visibility or handling, better that you find them out now than when you've handed the cash over!

Dealer

With a dealership, you should ask for a test drive of at least an hour. Some dealers will want to come along with you while others will let you go off by yourself if you leave your driving licence and old car keys with them. If the dealer does come along with you don't be fazed and worry that they're 'judging' your driving – they'll be used to sitting alongside all sorts of people.

If the dealership doesn't have the particular model you're interested in, they might encourage you to try another one – if you go ahead, do bear in mind that it may well have a very different feel – a 1.2 engine will be noticeably different from a 1.4, for example.

Even if you can feel yourself falling in love with the car, this is a time to play it cool and not reveal what's known in the trade as your 'car-lust'. If the dealer doesn't know you've got your heart set on it, you'll be in a stronger position when it comes to haggling.

Private sale

With a private sale, sellers are going to be understandably reluctant to let a complete stranger drive off with their car. They'll also be a bit unenthusiastic when it comes to lengthy test drives as they'll be keen to get it over with and will probably have other commitments such as picking their daughter up from ballet class or having their tea. But it's a good idea to stretch it out for as long as you dare – your general levels of persuasiveness and ability to get your own way will be a significant factor here.

The haggling process

Most of us are unfamiliar with haggling. In the UK bargain-hunting is more about finding a pair of shoes marked down from £70 to £45 in the sales, or buying cheap DVDs on eBay. Actually negotiating a lower price with a salesperson is something you might do in the souk on holiday, but not in everyday life. However, when it comes to buying a car, haggling can be an essential part of the process. The exceptions are auction houses and some internet car sites – and you'll often find that car supermarkets don't have the same haggling culture as dealerships.

It's during the haggling process that the research you've done previously will really pay off. If you've already got an idea of the target price for the car you're interested in and the trade-in one for your old model then you'll know where you stand and it'll be difficult for a dealer to, say, make you an excessively low trade-in offer on your old car.

And it'll also mean that when it comes to getting a bargain, your aims are realistic and achievable. If a car is offered at £15,000 and the *What Car?* target price is £14,500 then you've got something realistic to aim for – but marching into a dealership and expecting them to sell you a £15K car for £11K isn't going to get you anywhere, no matter how good your negotiating skills.

And finally, whether you're talking to a Ferrari dealership or someone selling their old Daewoo, aim to maintain a pleasant rapport. You'll get a better deal that way and, given that at a franchised dealership the salesperson may well be your first port of call for repairs and warranty issues, it's good to keep them onside.

Dealership

It's at the franchised dealership that the whole haggling issue has the biggest impact. Part of the reason is because larger sums of money are likely to be changing hands and also because there are often a lot of different balls being kept in the air – there's the cost of the car itself and the different extras and then possibly the issues of car finance and part-exchanging your old car as well.

It's a good idea to try and keep the deal as 'clear' as possible by just focusing on the cost of the car initially. Respond to any queries about finance or part-exchange by saying that you haven't decided what you're going to do yet.

This means that keeping them thinking they might be able to sell you a profitable finance deal will make them more keen to clinch a deal with you. And leaving the trade-in price of your car until last means that when you're discussing it it'll be in terms of actual cash, as opposed to the value somehow getting lost in the confusing whirl of special offers being made on finance deals and extras being 'thrown in'.

Bargaining chips

As haggling progresses you'll find that various 'bargaining chips' are bandied about – they can include items ranging from free air conditioning or a lower interest rate to free road tax, footwell mats or a full tank of petrol.

It's important to find out the cash value of these items

beforehand so you're not overcome by your dealer's 'generosity' in offering something that perhaps isn't of that much worth to you really.

One issue that's particularly worth exploring is that of free insurance – if you're an experienced driver with an unblemished record then that might only amount to a few hundred pounds. But if you're a new driver it can run into thousands and be far more valuable to you.

Shopping around is one of the most valuable weapons in your armoury – don't buy at the first place you visit, get some quotes from different dealers and use them to play them off against each other.

Private sale

The private seller is likely to be as keen to get the haggling process over and done with as you are. They'll have put the value of their car slightly above what they're willing to accept in the advert, expecting you to then play the game and say, 'would you accept xxx?' when you're making an offer and that'll be that. But do bear in mind that some sellers will have set the price at the market value (which you will of course have researched) anyway and there won't be the same room for manoeuvre. And then, of course, there are others who will have set it considerably above, either because they don't know what the true value of the car is or because they fancy themselves as hard-nosed business types. Whether you go along with their fixed price or walk away depends on you and how much you want this particular car. Incidentally, it's worth bearing in mind that some private sellers might try telling you a hard-luck story (which may or may not be true) about how badly they need the money when negotiating. It's a good idea not to let yourself be too swayed by this and only buy the car if you were going to anyway.

Paying for the car

The exchange of large sums of money for a car can be unnerving for both parties, especially when it comes to a private sale. If you withdraw large sums of cash from the bank there's the worry that you might get robbed or that the seller might run off with it. If you go down this route always have someone else with you and get the other person to check the money in front of you so that they can't claim the full amount wasn't there.

Cheques can be tricky as the seller probably won't want you to take the car away until the cheque has cleared – but then, unless you feel confident that the person is who they say they are, there's also the slight worry that they might abscond with your money and the car.

A banker's draft is usually a good option – this acts as proof that the money has been set aside and payment will be honoured by the bank. It's important to get a written, dated receipt from the seller with full details of the car (age, make, model, registration number, Vehicle Identification Number, mileage) and the sum that you've paid recorded in full.

It's also important to make sure that all the necessary paperwork is done to ensure that ownership of the vehicle is transferred from the dealer or previous owner to you.

Taking delivery of the car

By this stage you're probably feeling very impatient and eager to get behind the wheel of your new car and drive it away. But there are a few final hurdles of paperwork and checking still to clear. And whatever you do, read the handbook to learn about the basic controls before you set off – apparently a surprising number of accidents happen as the buyer is just setting off in their new car because they're distracted by fumbling with an unfamiliar dashboard.

Dealership

If you've ordered a new car it'll be delivered to the dealership and given a pre-delivery inspection (PDI). Then there's usually a handover when the dealer will talk you through various aspects of the car, give you the documents and provide any key or radio security codes. Look out now for any aspect of the car that isn't exactly as you ordered it or for any damage that might have happened in transit, such as scratches – mistakes can happen and it's going to be much easier to sort them out now than after you've driven it away.

Private sale

One last looking-over is a good idea and this is the time to be very firm about getting all the paperwork, the driver's manual and so on. You really don't want to be to-ing and fro-ing about this in the future.

But I'm not happy with my car!

Hopefully you'll skip this stage, be completely delighted with your car and have a long and trouble-free life together. But sometimes problems do occur shortly after you've bought it. The extent to which you've got any sort of legal comeback varies – but the more swiftly you act the better.

Dealership

It's best to go back to them as soon as possible and explain what's gone wrong. Most dealers will sort it out with you without any fuss and indeed be used to this sort of situation – it's usual for cars to have a few teething problems.

If you need to take things further then in the case of a franchised dealer contact the manufacturer's customer service department.

If the dealership is a member of a professional body, such as the Society of Motor Manufacturers and Traders, then get in touch with them. And if there's no progress there then it's the Citizens Advice Bureau or the Which? Legal Service.

Private sale

Unfortunately, unless you can prove that the seller misrepresented the car to you – such as lying about its mileage or previous history – your legal comeback is minimal and you're just going to have to accept that you bought a pig in a poke!

Chapter 9

Car Insurance Uncovered

As far as disagreeable but necessary obligations go, sorting out your car insurance is right up there with filling in tax returns, going for gynaecological check-ups or visiting dreary in-laws. But as with all these experiences, the best approach is just to grit your teeth, remind yourself that it'll be over soon and plan a nice treat for afterwards.

Sorting out car insurance can be a bewildering experience for many of us.

> *Car insurance is a mystery to me – it seems to consist of asking you a shedload of questions and then plucking a (generally big) number out of the sky.* Laura, 24

But you can make it much easier by getting up to speed on the terms insurers use and the sometimes sensible and sometimes twisted reasoning behind the questions they ask. This will help you both to get the right policy for your needs and to avoid paying too much for it.

Decoding insurance speak

⚙ Insurance premium – This is the cost of insuring your car. It can vary hugely depending on factors such as your age, driving experience, where you live and the type of car. If you're a new driver or live in an area with a high crime rate you could end up paying more for a year's car insurance than you did for your car – very depressing!

⊕ Cover note – This acts as a temporary policy and certificate until your new insurance policy has been fully set up.

⊕ Certificate of insurance –This is your formal evidence of insurance and you should get it shortly after taking your policy out. You'll need this to buy your road-tax disc.

⊕ Policy document – This is the document full of confusing small print that sets out the full terms and conditions of your policy. Mistakes and misunderstandings can turn out to be very expensive further down the line. It's important to read it carefully and call up the company for an explanation if there's anything you don't fully understand. Even if there are a zillion other things you would rather be doing.

⊕ The policyholder – The main driver of the car.

⊕ Named driver – This is an extra driver who uses the car less than the main driver. Usually the named driver can use it for leisure but not regular commuting.

⊕ 'Fronting' – This is a slang term for a bad thing that you must never do. It's when a more experienced driver puts themselves down as the main driver of a car and a less experienced one as a 'named driver' – even though the newer driver uses it more. Parents will sometimes do this for children who've just passed their test. This arrangement can be cheaper in terms of insurance costs but it's actually fraud. If you ever need to make a claim, insurance companies will investigate the situation and if they realize that 'fronting' has been going on then your policy can be declared invalid. You'll then be responsible for all the costs of the accident yourself and could also find it difficult to get insurance in the future.

Types of cover

- ⊖ Third party – Third party insurance covers your legal liability to pay damages to other people for injury to themselves, their passengers and their property. It is the minimum insurance you need to legally drive in the UK and it doesn't pay out for damage to your car or your medical expenses if you're injured. However, if the accident is proven to be the other party's fault their insurance should pay.
- ⊖ Third party fire and theft – This gives the above cover and will also pay out if your car is stolen or catches fire.
- ⊖ Fully comprehensive – This covers your liability to a third party, fire and theft. It also covers damage to you and your own car. It should pay for any repairs or a replacement car if yours is written off.

Some insurance companies will only authorize repairs by a garage named by them (approved repairers). This can be convenient as it means you don't have to trail around for quotes. However, if you would much rather stay loyal to your own garage then you might prefer a policy which allows you to decide where repairs are carried out.

It's important to be aware that if your car is written off or stolen, you won't necessarily get what you paid for it. It's more usual to be offered the 'current market value' for a car of that age and type.

Additional cover

Here are some other benefits which could be included in your policy, or which you might want to arrange as 'add-on' cover.

- ⊛ Motor legal expenses – This will cover your legal expenses if, for example, you're involved in an accident that isn't your fault and you need to claim your uninsured losses, such as your excess or the cost of a replacement car, from the other party.

- ⊛ Temporary replacement car – Sometimes referred to as a 'courtesy car'. If having your car off the road after an accident would cause you serious problems then you might want to take out cover that would provide you with a car while your own is being repaired or replaced.

- ⊛ Personal belongings – If you regularly travel with a suitcase full of designer clothes or carry expensive sports equipment or your laptop in your car you might want to consider being insured against their theft. However, these items could already be covered on your home insurance policy, so check that first. There's no point in insuring things twice!

- ⊛ 'Driving other cars' insurance – This covers the policyholder when driving other people's cars with their permission – but cover is generally limited to third party only, and only in emergency situations.

- ⊛ Breakdown cover – Some insurance companies will encourage you to take out breakdown cover with them as well. However, this might not be the best deal for you – shop around and get some quotes from breakdown companies such as the AA or RAC.

Excess

Excess comes in three varieties – compulsory, voluntary and
'young driver excess'. Basically, it's the amount that you have
to pay on any insurance claim before the insurance company's
contribution kicks in. Compulsory excess is set by the insurer,
but you can offer to pay more – that is, a voluntary excess in
exchange for a lower premium. However, setting your voluntary excess too high can mean that you avoid claiming in an
accident and so may turn out to be a false economy. Insurers
almost always make young drivers pay an extra 'young driver
excess' on top of the standard compulsory excess – typically
it's an extra £250 until 21, then reducing to an extra £150
until 25.

No-claims discount (sometimes called no-claims bonus)

If you don't claim on your insurance for a number of years,
insurance companies will begin to see you as a safer bet, and
start offering you a discount on your insurance. Discounts vary
between insurers but it can reach a maximum of about 60 per
cent after five or six years. So a basic insurance premium of say
£700 can be reduced to £280 – it's savings like these that make
people so keen on their no-claims discount and so willing to
jump through hoops to protect it.

Signing up for a no-claims discount is another area where it's
important to check the small print – some companies will only

allow you to claim for one accident a year, while others will allow more than that.

As a general rule you can only build up your no-claims discount when you're driving your own car, rather than being a named driver on someone else's. However, some companies, such as Directline, are beginning to offer this. It's also sometimes possible to get one based on company car experience.

Factors that influence the cost of car insurance

1. The type of cover

As you might expect, fully comprehensive is the most expensive. If you're a young or inexperienced driver then the cost can be very high. And if your car is an old banger then getting insurance cover to repair it or replace it if it's stolen might actually end up costing more than the car is worth – which may well mean that third party would be a better bet.

Many new drivers start off with third party and then work up to fully comprehensive when they've had a few years' experience and their insurance becomes cheaper.

However, if you do go for third party only, you might want to consider having add-on cover for motor legal expenses to supplement it. It's also worth getting quotes for additional benefits you'd like, such as a replacement car, and weighing up whether they're important enough to you to fork out for.

Your cover as a named driver

If you're insuring your own car, the type of cover you go for is up to you. If you're going on someone else's insurance as a named driver you'll generally be offered the same sort of cover (third party fire and theft, fully comprehensive, etc.) that they have. If you want any changes or supplements then discuss this with the insurance company to see if that's possible.

2. The car

The insurance group (ABI group)

Whenever a new car is developed, the manufacturers deliver sample models for testing at the insurance industry's test centre. Safety features such as airbags and seat designs are evaluated, they look at how the car performs in crash tests, the engine power, the cost of repairs and parts and security features such as alarms and immobilizers. Then a panel of experts agrees a group rating. The insurance groups currently go from 1 to 20 – the lowest being the cheaper cars to insure. Although a lot of factors are taken into consideration, basically the high-performance cars and those that would be more attractive to car thieves are in the higher groups. Here are some examples:

- Citroën 2CV – group 1
- Ford Focus – about 4–8
- A 'hot hatchback' (a small hatchback car with a powerful engine) such as a VW Golf Gti – about 14–15
- Porsche 911 Carrera – 20

You can find the insurance group rating of a car on the manufacturer's website or at www.parkers.co.uk or www.glass.co.uk.

Age of the car

It is generally assumed that older cars are cheaper to insure, but that's not always the case. Some older cars can be difficult to get replacement parts for, which makes them more expensive to repair. And as some of them aren't as responsive as newer cars they can be more accident-prone. More recent cars are also much safer in terms of protecting passengers. But on the other hand there are older cars where cover is very reasonable. The only way to find out which category a car falls into is to get a quote specifically for it.

Security features

The more you can protect your car against theft, the lower your premium is likely to be. Keeping it in a garage or on a driveway overnight is seen as a definite plus. Getting a car alarm or steering lock fitted can help lower your premium – but you do have to commit to using them every time you leave your car unattended, because if you don't and it's stolen then your policy won't be valid.

Modifications

A car that's had modifications such as alloy wheels, tinted windows or spoilers fitted is likely to be more expensive to insure. This is because these 'pimping your ride' type of alterations are associated with boy racers. They also make the car more attractive to the sort of thieves who'll want to drive it round like a nutcase then set fire to it in a car park.

3. You

Your age

Getting older has its drawbacks – hangovers get worse and you start taking rather too much interest in the spurious 'collagen-enhancing with magical penetrating liposomes' claims of anti-ageing cream manufacturers. But on the upside, your car insurance gets cheaper. Statistically, younger people have more accidents, so between 17 and 20 you're seen as being particularly high-risk. At 21 premiums take a significant drop, and then again at 25.

Your gender

There are many reasons to enjoy being a girl – not least that our car insurance is cheaper. This is because of our admirable safety record compared to men. Though as it happens, women do have roughly as many accidents as men. The difference is that women's accidents tend to be of the 'reversing into bollards' variety, whereas men are more likely to get involved in high-speed motorway accidents in which cars need extensive repairs or are even written off.

Where you live

If you live in an area with a high crime rate your premium is going to be higher than if you're in a more law-abiding one because you're at greater risk of having your car stolen. Areas where there's a higher density of traffic also attract higher premiums, as it's more likely that you're going to bump into another car going round the M25 than when driving through the Scottish Highlands. For example, a 25–45-year-old living in East London and insuring a Ford Focus Zetec will on average be paying £315, compared to just £116 in Dundee.

If you divide your time between two places – for example, you're a student spending part of the year at university in Birmingham and part of it back home with your parents in some sleepy backwater – then you might be tempted to choose the cheaper address and give that one to the insurance company as it'll make your premium much cheaper. Don't though.

If you need to make a claim, the insurance company will almost certainly manage to work out your ruse and use it as an excuse to render your policy invalid and wriggle out of paying anything at all. When you call up for a quote explain the situation and ask for the fact that you divide your time between the two locations to be taken into consideration.

Your mileage

A common mistake that people make when applying for car insurance is either over- or under-estimating their mileage – meaning that they end up either paying too much or rendering their policy invalid because of exceeding their stated mileage. The internet application forms and telephone salespeople will often offer an average distance of about 12,000 miles, but it's important to find out if you do significantly more or less than this. You can work it out by looking at old MOT certificates, seeing how far you've driven in previous years and estimating whether that's likely to change, or getting out a pocket calculator and working out your likely distances.

What you use your car for: 'Type of use'

The three main types of use are 'social, domestic and pleasure', 'commuting' and 'business'. It's important to be accurate about the 'type of use' when taking out a policy and allow for times when that might change. For example, if you mostly commute by train, but might use your car occasionally, it's still important to put down 'commute' as well as 'business' and 'pleasure' – because otherwise if you're involved in an accident on your way to work, you won't be covered.

Your occupation

Insurance companies often take occupation into consideration when calculating premiums. If you're a journalist or a burlesque dancer then you're seen as being more likely to drink and drive and do a lot of night driving and hence be more at risk. If on the other hand you've got a rather more sedate profession such as a bank clerk then you're viewed as a safer prospect.

Your driving history

If you've had accidents in the past or have points on your licence, your premiums are likely to be higher. Just one speeding conviction can add £200 to your annual premium. If you've been convicted of a major driving offence, such as drink-driving, then you're in serious trouble – your insurance is going to cost a fortune. Insurers might also only offer you limited cover – they'll insure you for third party but refuse to take you on for fully comprehensive.

If you're a young or relatively new driver then having older, more experienced drivers on the policy can bring it down – even if the named driver only drives it infrequently, it's seen as levelling out the risk. Definitely look into this when you're getting quotes.

Whether you've got sat nav

Some insurance companies will give you a lower quote if you've got sat nav, based on the theory that satellite navigation makes you safer on the road because your attention is focused on your driving rather than fretting about whether you've just missed your motorway junction.

Taking the Pass Plus course

For new drivers, taking a Pass Plus course after your driving test can help bring down your insurance. This is an extra set of training sessions you take after you've passed your test and covers skills such as motorway and night driving. It takes six hours or sometimes slightly more, doesn't have an exam at the end and needs to be taught by a suitably qualified instructor. The cost is about £150 and many insurers offer insurance discounts of up to 30 per cent for new drivers who have taken this extra set of training sessions. It can also give you cheaper insurance as a named driver.

Choosing your car insurance

Many people choose their car insurance by logging onto an internet site, plugging in their details, looking at the cheapest quote that pings up and going for that one. That isn't necessarily the best route to take, however. 'Don't just buy on price, buy on policy,' advises Malcolm Tarling of the Association of British Insurers. 'Make sure that you're not agreeing to an excessively high level of excess in return for a cheaper premium, or leaving out some aspect of cover, such as personal belongings, that would be important to you.'

When it comes to sorting out car insurance, the internet is your friend. The websites www.confused.com and www.comparethemarket.com are both excellent, and can help you find the best deal.

Getting organized beforehand will make the process a lot quicker and easier. Dig out all the documents you'll need, the details of the car you want insured (or the several cars you might want to check out before deciding which to buy), your expected mileage and the level of cover you're after.

Always make sure you compare 'like with like' – Insurer A might make you an offer that's cheaper than insurer B but which doesn't include something that's important to you, such as insurance for your personal belongings.

Don't assume you'll get a better quote from a company that specializes in women drivers. All insurers factor the statistics about women being safer drivers into their calculations.

When you're trying to bring your quote down, try out different scenarios such as 'What if I fitted a car alarm?' 'What if I had my partner on as a named driver?' and see what effect it has on your premium.

Avoid paying in monthly instalments if you possibly can. Essentially, what the company is doing is loaning you the full amount upfront and then charging you a high rate (often up to 20 per cent) of interest on it. If you do need to take out a loan for your premium you'll be able to find a much better deal by shopping around for one.

Don't leave sorting out your car insurance till the last minute – that way you'll have plenty of time to decide what cover you need, do your research thoroughly, indulge in a spot of haggling and end up with the best possible price.

If you change cars

If your car has to be scrapped or you decide to sell it then cancelling your policy can involve an admin charge of about £50. However, if you're planning on buying another one soon then ask the insurer if it's possible to keep the policy running till then (often called suspending cover) as this can work out more cost-effective.

Making a car insurance claim

Claiming on your own car insurance isn't too complicated – so if, say, you've accidentally scraped someone else's car and need to pay for the damage, then sorting out a payment for this should be fairly straightforward.

However, problems can arise when your own insurance is third party, but you were involved in an accident that was the other person's fault and you want to claim off their insurance. 'If they admit it, then everything will be fine,' says insurance expert Malcolm Tarling. 'But human nature being what it is, people will sometimes contest your version of events. That's why it's so important to gather as much information as possible at the time of an accident – get the names and contact details of witnesses, take photographs of any damage or skid marks. To be able to successfully claim on someone else's insurance you have to not just believe that they were negligent, but be able to prove it, which is why evidence is so vital.'

Your happily insured year ahead

Once you've finally got your car insurance sorted out, it's very tempting to just breathe a sigh of relief, shove the policy in a drawer and forget about it. But sadly you can't be complacent. In the course of a year changes to your circumstances may take place that could render your policy invalid if you don't inform the insurance company about them.

They include:

- moving house
- changing jobs
- developing a health problem that might affect your driving
- having to keep the car on the road rather than in a garage
- having an accident (even one you don't intend to claim for)
- getting points on your licence

and so on.

My cousin got points on her licence for speeding, didn't realize she had to tell her insurance company and it was only when she had a little crash that she realized she'd been driving round uninsured for the best part of a year. Martina, 30

If the change is significant enough for the policy to need to be re-drafted then you might have to pay an administration fee of about £20. It's annoying, but necessary to keep your car insurance valid. Make sure they confirm their acknowledgement and acceptance of any changes in writing.

Sorting out car insurance is such a drag that once you've signed up with a particular company it's tempting to stick with them when your policy comes up for renewal the following year. If you're an experienced driver with a good record living in a safe area then your insurance premium is likely to be fairly low anyway and shopping around might only shave off £20 or £30, so you may decide not to bother changing. But if you're a new driver or have a car in a high insurance group then there's a far greater chance of significant savings – one of the easiest options is to research quotes and then ask your current insurer if they'll match it. Often they'll agree, so you'll get the saving without the administrative hassle of changing companies.

Chapter 10

Driving Disasters

Driving can be challenging as well as fun. One minute you're cruising along without a care in the world, the next you're stuck by the roadside with a flat tyre. Or maybe the weather changes unexpectedly and you're left battling through a blizzard or edging your car through a real pea-souper of a fog.

Then there are the driving disasters which can't be blamed on bad luck or the forces of nature – it's more a case of Girls Behaving Badly. Speeding, driving over the alcohol limit and virtually all parking tickets fall into this category. And of course it's important to look after yourself – most women feel safer in their cars than on foot or public transport, but there can still be times when you might run into scary situations.

The advice in this chapter will help you tackle any driving disasters with confidence and style, keep you on the straight and narrow where your own driving is concerned and supply useful tips on personal safety for girls on the go.

Breakdowns

As always, prevention is better than cure. Making sure your car is serviced and checked regularly will help prevent breakdowns – but it's not infallible. 'Modern cars often take people by surprise when they break down,' says Adam Ashmore, AA patrolman of the year for 2007. 'Older cars – by which I mean those pre-1995 – often showed signs that they were ailing in advance – they'd make funny noises or be difficult to start in the mornings. However, modern cars tend to behave perfectly until something goes wrong and then they'll pack up when you least expect it.'

And of course it is one of the more infuriating laws of nature that breakdowns happen at the worst possible times. When you're going out and wearing your best clothes, for example. Or when there's a raging thunderstorm.

Fix it yourself or call for help?

One of the first things you'll be asking yourself when you break down is whether this is a situation you can sort out alone, or one where you need to call your breakdown service. The answer to that question can feel somewhat loaded. It's as if the ability to change a tyre has come to be seen as some sort of badge of honour and proof that you're an Independent Woman as opposed to being the sort of drippy girl who Needs a Man to Rescue Her.

But truly, there's no shame in calling the breakdown service. In recent years cars have become increasingly complex and run by sensitive electrical systems – systems that it's very easy to mess up if you don't know what you're doing. 'A little knowledge can be a dangerous thing,' says Adam Ashmore. 'If you're not totally sure of what you're doing then what used to be seen as a fairly straightforward procedure, such as jump-starting your car, can cause expensive damage.'

It's all about confidence, and confidence is born of familiarity. If you're already comfortable with doing the safety checks on your car and have changed wheels or charged up batteries in your own garage, then you'll probably be fine tackling some basic

Basic Breakdown Guidelines

Put your hazard warning lights on as soon as you can – that way other drivers will know you're in difficulties and give you a wide berth.

Think twice before accepting help from passing drivers – if anyone approaches you, get into your car and talk to them through a lowered window while you come to a decision.

Having breakdown equipment in the car can make all the difference to how easy breakdowns are to handle – having items like a jack and a wheelbrace means you've got the option of changing a tyre at the side of the road, for example.

A fully charged mobile phone – if it's pay-as-you-go, make sure you've got enough credit. It can be worth keeping a top-up voucher in the glove compartment just in case.

A torch – the sort you can recharge by winding it up or shaking it is best.

A hazard warning triangle.

Reflective jacket.

Waterproof clothes and walking shoes (if you can't get a signal on your phone and you have to walk through the snow for help you really don't want to be doing it in ballet pumps).

Bottled water and chocolate to eat in an emergency (if you're enough of a chocoholic to consider stopping at traffic lights to be 'an emergency' then keep it in the boot rather than the glove compartment or substitute for a less alluring snack such as Kendal's Mint Cake or one of those unappetizing energy bars you can buy in outdoor shops).

Possibly a tyre puncture repair kit, jump leads and a battery recharger.

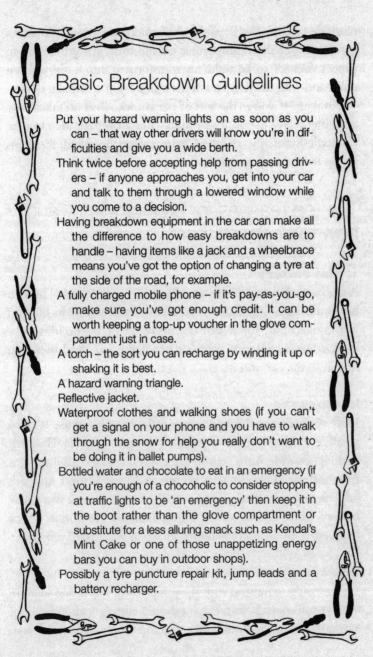

roadside repairs. But if you're profoundly unenthusiastic about getting under the bonnet most of the time, it's unrealistic to expect yourself to be suddenly transformed into a girl who's a dab hand with the jump leads the minute you've broken down.

Similarly, if you're the sort of person who lives on takeaways and microwave meals, it's probably not a brilliant idea to take on single-handedly cooking Christmas lunch with all the trimmings for a dozen people.

The top reasons for breakdowns – and how to deal with them

1. Flat battery

A flat battery is one of the top causes of breakdowns. This can happen because the battery has reached the end of its life and just conked out. Or it can be the result of overloading it – maybe leaving interior lights or headlights on. And then you return to the car and it's got a flat battery!

How to avoid it

Have your battery checked as part of its regular service. It's also possible to have free battery checks at some garages. Halfords and Nationwide Auto centres are good places to call into for a free battery check as they're regularly monitored and are unlikely to try the dodgy-garage trick of trying to sell you a new battery when you don't need one. And always double-check that you've turned all the lights off when you leave your car.

What to do if it happens to you

Unless you're a natural with the jump leads, this is one to leave to the professionals. In fact, you should even be cautious about letting a passing motorist offer to jump-start your car for you.

'It's so easy to damage the electrical systems of both cars,' says Adam Ashmore. 'Even disconnecting the leads in the wrong order can cause problems.'

2. Flat tyre

If you get a puncture you'll soon know about it – the steering will start to feel odd, the car will start to wander about and you might hear strange noises from the wheel as well. Pull over as soon as you can and inspect the damage. Another situation when you might be confronted by a flat tyre is when you return to your car and it is deflated because of earlier damage.

How to avoid it

Keep your tyres inflated to the correct pressure and inspect them regularly for signs of damage.

What to do if it happens to you

Don't try driving any distance with a flat tyre or puncture – it's dangerous and can damage your car. Small punctures can be repaired by inexpensive kits you can keep in the boot – one of the most popular is Holts Tyreweld at £7.99 – available from Halfords and www.me-mo.co.uk. It's an aerosol that you squirt through the tyre valve to seal the hole and inflate the tyre. It's only a temporary measure, and the manufacturer's guidelines will stipulate a top speed – probably about 50 m.p.h., which you need to stick to. But it can at least help you get home or to the nearest garage.

Or of course, you might decide to change the tyre yourself. But before you embark on this, it's important to be aware of the pitfalls. For example, the quality of the tools (wheel wrench and jack) you'll find in the boot might not be of very good quality. And it's usual for garages to tighten up wheel nuts very firmly, so getting them off can be a struggle. And then when you're replacing the wheel it's important to make sure it's not fitted either too loosely or too tightly. 'If the wheel studs are tightened up too much there's the risk of them stretching or snapping – if they're not tight enough then the wheel might fall off,' says Adam Ashmore. 'It's important that all the wheels are at the same level of tightness – that they're taken up to what's called a specific torque. To do this you need a torque wrench. If you don't have one with you then it's important to get the wheels balanced when you get home – either by yourself or at a garage.'

If you would like to be able to change your own tyres, then it's a good idea to go to a car maintenance class and have proper instruction. Alternatively at least have a few practice runs at home so your first attempt isn't when you're stressed out and at the side of a busy road.

Changing a tyre

- Pull as close to the kerb as possible – move off-road onto a lay-by if possible.
- Make sure the car is on a level surface as you shouldn't use the jack with the car at an angle.
- Put the handbrake and hazard warning lights on.
- Find the jack, the wheelbrace (for undoing wheel nuts) and spare wheel (they're normally in the boot under the boot carpet).
- Take off the hubcap or cover over the wheel nuts using the wheelbrace and loosen the wheel nuts slightly.
- Position the jack in the correct place (your car handbook will tell you exactly where) and jack up the car until the punctured tyre is off the ground.
- Take off the nuts and lift off the wheel – lift the spare into place and screw the wheel nuts back on.
- Lower the jack completely.
- Finish tightening up the wheel nuts with the wheelbrace.

As soon as you've completed your journey take the damaged wheel to a garage or tyre specialist for repair or replacement.

3. Key problems – it won't work!

If you've got a car key which opens your car remotely, there will be times when it doesn't work and you're locked out! The usual reason for this is that the battery in the fob has run out.

How to avoid it

The battery in your key fob will need to be replaced at intervals, so find out when it needs doing and ask your garage to replace it when the car is in for a service.

What to do if it happens to you

Technically, it should be possible to buy a replacement battery from a car accessories shop. But unfortunately even if you're able to do that the key will sometimes need reprogramming before you can use it (it's all about those electrical systems again!). Reprogramming instructions will be in the driver's handbook.

4. Key problems – you've locked them in the car!

As you tend to need your keys to lock your car, actually shutting them in there can involve quite a complicated sequence of events – but people do manage it! 'Often people will do something like lock their car, put the key in their coat pocket then put the coat in the boot and slam it shut,' says Adam Ashmore.

How to avoid it

Think things through carefully – and if you're the forgetful type then make sure you've got a spare set tucked away in your handbag.

What to do if it happens to you

Breaking into your car isn't a good idea and can even damage it. Your best bet is to call your breakdown service, who will have a database of ways to open the door and be able to get into most cars. They may offer to drive you home if you've got a spare set there and it's not too far.

5. Key problems – you've lost them!

Losing your keys doesn't technically count as a breakdown, but it does mean that you can't get into your car or go anywhere, so you're pretty stuck!

How to avoid it

Always keep your keys in the same place – and take care of your possessions so your handbag or purse containing your keys doesn't get stolen.

What to do if it happens

Call a family member or friend and ask them to bring the spare keys to you. If you don't have any spare keys you'll have to go along to the dealership for your make of car, together with documents to prove you own it, such as the V5, and give them the VIN (vehicle identification number) and proof of your identity. It can be expensive though – brace yourself for a bill of £100, maybe even more.

6. Misfuelling

About 120,000 motorists fill their tanks with the wrong fuel every year. Putting diesel in a petrol tank is bad enough, but it's petrol in a diesel tank that can do the most serious damage.

How to avoid it
Always check the pumps carefully, especially if you're away from home. You can get used to the ones at your local garage but end up getting it wrong when you're confronted with unfamiliar ones, particularly if you're tired during a long journey.

What to do if it happens to you
Don't start the car, whatever you do – the mix of fuel can really damage your engine! Get someone to help you push your vehicle away from the pumps and call your breakdown service, who will drain the fuel system for you.

7. Running out of fuel
This is an astonishingly common problem. Sometimes it's just the result of pure carelessness and forgetting to check the fuel gauge. Other times it's because the fuel gauge itself is faulty and was reading full when it was actually empty. Alternatively there could be a fuel leak.

How to avoid it
If you suspect that the fuel gauge is playing up, or that you've got a leak of any description, get it checked out by a garage as soon as possible. And don't procrastinate when it comes to filling up.

What to do if it happens to you
If you suspect a fuel leak then you should be able to smell the petrol or diesel. Don't even think of trying to start the car under these circumstances – call the breakdown service for help.

Don't keep attempting to start the engine in the hope of squeezing the last drops of fuel out as this can suck air and dirt into the fuel system and make things even worse.

If you've got a can of fuel with you or can get one from a nearby petrol station then switch off the ignition, empty it into the tank and drive to the nearest garage to fill up properly.

If you're stuck on the hard shoulder or a long way from the nearest petrol station then your best bet is to call your breakdown service.

8. Overheated engine

When the car overheats the most likely reason is that there's not enough coolant in the radiator – maybe because there's a leak or maybe because it hasn't been topped up properly. However, there can be more complicated reasons, such as a problem with the cylinder head gasket.

How to avoid it

Having your car serviced at the proper intervals and checking the coolant levels regularly will reduce the chances of this problem occurring.

What to do if it happens to you

'A lot of people think that all they need to do if their engine overheats is to top up the coolant with water and drive on,' says Adam Ashmore of the AA.

But it's not as simple as that – you need to find out why the coolant level is so low. Normally it's because some other part of the engine has failed and so, even if you do top up, the car will only break down again five miles down the road, by which time you could have done some serious damage to it. It's best to pull over and lift up the bonnet to let the engine cool. But don't open the radiator cap unless the engine is completely cold. Otherwise the combination of the heat and pressure means that you'll be sprayed with a mixture of scalding water and toxic coolant – it's nasty! When we do it at the AA we use protective clothing and goggles, otherwise there's the risk of serious injury.

So, this is another time to call your breakdown service.

Location, location

Car breakdowns are always a drag – but some locations are worse to break down in than others. The most convenient is, of course, at home. If you want to try repairing any problem yourself you'll have your garage and tools nearby. And if you want to call your garage or breakdown service you can go inside and have a cup of tea while you do it.

If you can sense problems developing with your car when you're driving in a town or residential area it's a good idea to try and make it to a pub car park or at least a quiet residential street. That way it will be easier to check out your car away from busy traffic – and you'll have the option of sitting and waiting for the breakdown patrol over an orange juice in the pub rather than in your car.

Breaking down on a rural road can be hazardous – especially if it's on a bend. Some country roads don't have much traffic and people who drive along them regularly often don't expect to meet other vehicles – especially not ones that have broken down. This is one of the situations where having a hazard warning triangle can come in particularly useful.

The motorway is the most dangerous place to break down. If you do, pull over to the hard shoulder, get out of the nearside door and go to the other side of the barrier. The suction from fast cars and lorries as they pass by can be very strong, so be prepared for it. The reason why it's so dangerous to stay put is because the drivers of other vehicles who may not be concentrating properly might see your car and assume it's the far-left lane, line up behind it and plough into the back of your stationary car.

Call your breakdown organization and let them know where you are – it's important not even to consider trying to repair your car on the hard shoulder. This is a job best left to the professionals. If you don't have a mobile phone then use one of the call boxes on the hard shoulder – you don't need cash for it and it will go straight through to the police, who will advise you what to do. And it sounds so obvious – but don't ever try to cross the carriageway – this is incredibly dangerous.

Different types of accidents and how to cope with them

The accident with the lowest hassle quotient is the type where you damage your own car but nothing else. For example, you reverse into a bollard. The bollard emerges unscathed but one of your rear lights is smashed.

In this instance there's no one you need to exchange addresses with, it's just a case of getting the light repaired. Even if you're not going to claim off your insurance you ought to let your company know as it's almost certainly a condition of your policy to inform them of any mishaps.

The next step up is if you damage someone else's property – you reverse into their fence or scrape their stationary vehicle, for example. What you're then meant to do is to track down the owner of the property. In the case of the fence then it's just a case of going up the garden path to the house, but the owners of parked cars can be trickier to track down. However, it's a legal requirement to at least make an effort – try knocking on a few doors, or going into nearby coffee shops and asking, 'Does anyone in here own the red Seat Ibiza parked outside?', all the time praying the scary Gillian McKeith lookalike at the corner table isn't going to be the person to answer yes.

If you can't find the owner then you should put a note with your name and contact details on their windscreen. And if you've got a camera or cameraphone with you, then it's a good idea to take a picture of your car and theirs – you don't want to end up paying for damage that's already there, or for anything that might happen afterwards.

Injury to animals

Running over any animal is upsetting. From a legal standpoint you're meant to report any dead or injured dogs, but it's not required that you do so for cats. But, of course, it's best to let the police and the local RSPCA shelter know so at least their owner will know what happened rather than spending ages searching for them.

Accident checklist

Accidents are horrible, confusing events and it can be difficult to think straight during them. That's why it's a good idea to have an 'accident checklist' covering things that you should do or record during an accident. Some insurance companies issue them or have them on their website, so if yours does then it's a good idea to keep a copy in your glove compartment. Here's a sample checklist.

Is everyone concerned OK?

The top priority in any accident is the well-being of the people concerned. If anyone's been injured or is in a state of shock then it's important to call an ambulance.

The guidelines as regards first aid are:

- ☣ Don't move injured people unless absolutely necessary.
- ☣ Don't ever remove a crash helmet.
- ☣ If someone is bleeding, press a clean cloth onto the wound, raising the wound as you do so.
- ☣ If someone is in shock, keep them warm.

Stay calm

Feelings can run high at the scene of an accident but it's important to stay calm. If anyone else involved gets scary and road-ragey then call the police.

What records should I take?

- ☣ Make a note of the time.
- ☣ Make a note of any injuries suffered by you or anyone else.
- ☣ Make a note of the damage to your car, the other person's car, any other vehicles or property such as fencing.
- ☣ If there are any witnesses, ask for their details. They might refuse, but it's worth a try. If you've got a camera or cameraphone, take photos of both cars – both their positioning, any skid marks and any damage they might have sustained.

⊖ Make sketches if you can.

⊖ Make a note of everything you can remember (the speed you were going at, the weather, any other vehicles around at the time, road signs such as give way or stop signs).

⊖ If any police officers come to the scene, then make a note of their names and numbers.

What details should I get or give?

⊖ Driver's full name (also the details of the owner of the car, if they are different)

⊖ address

⊖ telephone number

⊖ insurance details – company and policy number, if they have it

⊖ vehicle registration

⊖ colour, make and model of the vehicle

Bear in mind that 1 in 20 drivers on the road is uninsured – the person involved in this accident might be one of them. This means that they might be giving you false information of the 'My name is Alice Adams and I live at 11 Acacia Avenue' variety. If you suspect this might be the case, make a note of other identifying things such as a physical description of the person and their car. If the police are at the scene it would be worth mentioning it to them or if you haven't phoned them till this point then it would be worth making a discreet call and asking them to attend the accident.

An uninsured driver might also suggest that you 'sort this out between ourselves' and don't get the insurance company involved, but you shouldn't go along with this – it's better to do things by the book, as the other person could come back to you later and ask for more money for the damage than they originally mentioned. Going through your insurance company will protect your interests if things get awkward further down the line.

Never admit or deny liability at the scene of an accident – there is usually a term to this effect in your insurance policy. If you're the sort of person who apologizes when someone else stands on your foot, resisting the urge to take the blame can feel difficult – but stay neutral at this point and let it be sorted out through the official channels.

What should I do afterwards?

Don't drive!

Even if your car is driveable, please don't travel anywhere in it. You'll be shaken and need time to calm down before getting behind the wheel again, so take it easy. Ideally get a friend or family member to come and pick you up, or order a cab to take you home.

Contact your insurance company

Contact your insurance company as soon as possible and they'll be able to guide you through the next steps.

If you've only got third party insurance and the collision wasn't your fault you can claim from whoever was legally liable for the damage. However, you'll have to be able to prove their negligence beyond reasonable doubt, so the more back-up information you can acquire at the time, the better.

Even if the driver is uninsured you can still claim via the Motor Insurers' Bureau which is a government body – again, your insurance company will advise you on this.

My car's been stolen!

Yet another situation where prevention is better than cure. Try to always park your car in a safe, well-lit area or in a car park with an attendant. You might also want to invest in a car alarm or in a steering wheel lock – most thieves want an easy life and if they can see that nicking your motor will present a challenge, they're more likely to leave it alone.

Before you jump to the conclusion that your car has been stolen, check out the other possibilities first. First – are you absolutely sure that you've returned to where you left it. Some car parks, such as multi-storeys and those at festivals can be very confusing, so do a thorough search for your car before calling the police. You should also check with family and friends who have spare keys that they haven't taken the car. Another possibility is that it could have been towed away for a parking or obstruction offence – so check out if there are any warning notices with contact phone numbers on them that you could call.

If it really has been stolen, then it's time to phone the police – they'll need the following information:

- your name and address
- the make, colour and registration number of your car
- where you left your car and what time, when you returned
- details of any valuable items you left in the car

Call your insurance company as soon as possible and give them the same details – if you've got problems getting home without your car then check if you're covered for travel by either them or your breakdown organization.

If your car hasn't been stolen but has been broken into, call the police and your insurance company. Don't assume that your car is safe to drive – the ignition or electrical wiring systems may have been tampered with, so it's best to get it checked out before getting behind the wheel.

Driving in difficult conditions

Driving disasters are more likely to happen when the weather conditions are challenging or at night. Here are some tips for dealing with these situations.

Night driving

There's no doubt that driving at night is more dangerous. A Department of Transport study in 2004 revealed that although only about 15 per cent of vehicle miles are clocked between 7 p.m. and 7 a.m., they account for almost a third of road injuries and deaths. This is because of reduced visibility and because there are more drivers on the road under the influence of drink or drugs.

It's worth bearing in mind that there are lots of different sorts of night driving – cruising along at 30 m.p.h. in a built-up area with lots of street lamps is a different matter from driving along a pitch-black country lane and different again from a busy dual carriageway, being dazzled by oncoming headlights and under pressure from drivers behind to go faster.

To stay safe make sure your lights and windows are clean – this makes a tremendous difference. Even if you feel hassled to go faster by other drivers, only go at a speed where you can stop safely within the distance you can see in your headlights.

Winter motoring

Driving in the winter can be anything from a drag to downright daunting. If you're a city girl there's not too much reason to worry about getting caught in a snowdrift – but iced-up windscreens and frozen locks can still be a problem. And if you live in the countryside then there's the challenge of driving on icy roads and the risk of worst-case scenarios such as getting stranded in the snow. Here are some tips for keeping you driving in a winter wonderland.

Preparing your car for winter

Breakdowns are more common in winter than at any other time. One of the main reasons for this is that extra strain is being put on the battery. Having to start in cold conditions is bad enough, and then you'll also be using more equipment such as the heating, de-misters and headlights, all of which draw on the battery power. After Christmas is a particular high spot for battery failure as people enthusiastically plug all the iPods or DVD players they've been given as presents into the system.

It's especially important to have a battery that's in tip-top condition during this time. If it shows any signs of ill health, such as problems with starting first thing in the morning, then get your car to a garage for a battery check. Garages that offer 'free battery checks' might just end up trying to sell you a new battery when you don't actually need one. Going to a garage you trust or one of the chains like Halfords or Nationwide Auto will bypass this – they're monitored regularly and won't try to diddle you!

Sometimes run-down batteries can be recharged with a battery charger or by jump-starting – but if your battery is playing up regularly then it's a sign that it's on its way out. If possible it's a good idea to time your car's service for just before the winter as this will be an opportunity for your garage to check the battery and that you've got the correct water:antifreeze ratio in your coolant.

It's also especially important to do the regular safety checks outlined in Chapter 4, 'Keep Your Motor Running', during the winter. And good visibility is vital so make sure your headlights are working properly and that your windows are all clean.

Useful winter items
As well as the usual breakdown items, it can be a good idea to have an ice-scraper, de-icing spray and maybe jump leads or a power pack for recharging your battery. You might also need a shovel (it's possible to buy fold-up shovels, which don't take up as much space) and cat litter (to put under the wheels if you get stuck).

Before setting off
Always allow more time for winter motoring – take into account that you'll have to de-ice the windows at the very least, and also that you'll probably need more time for your journey.

Listen to the weather reports and don't set off if they're really bad. If you're driving in a rural area always tell someone where you're going and what route you'll be taking.

It's especially important to keep your tank topped up in winter – fuel consumption soars in cold weather.

In parts of the UK with extreme weather conditions such as Scotland, snow chains or studded tyres can be a good idea. Talk to colleagues and neighbours about whether they find them useful and ask for advice on how to get them fitted.

Icy windscreen

Icy windscreens are the bane of the winter motorist. One good 'prevention is better than cure' strategy is to invest in a thin windscreen cover – they cost about £5 and are kept in place by the car doors. In the morning, you just whisk it off!

When you're de-icing your windows it's important to do it properly – it's not OK to set off with just a tiny letterbox-shaped hole in your windscreen to peer through and tell yourself that the other windows will defrost as you drive along. You need to do all of them thoroughly. Ice-scrapers and de-icing spray (you can get eco-friendly ones or make your own with water and vinegar) will help sort your windows out. It's also not a good idea to set the engine running and then leave the car to defrost. Quite apart from the fact it's a waste of fuel and bad for the battery it's also a classic route for thieves to steal cars – insurers call it 'frosting'.

Frozen locks

If you find that your car locks freeze overnight, one useful tip is to put masking tape over the locks in the evening – it'll stop the moisture getting in. WD40, a lubricant available at all car accessory shops, is excellent for removing water from locks so ice can't form – just insert the plastic tube into the lock and give it a good squirt. Another alternative is to nip indoors, run your key under the hot tap and then rush back out again and see if the hot key will help the ice melt more quickly.

Winter driving dos and don'ts

If the weather is snowy or icy then it's especially important to stay alert. Even if this is a run you do every day, don't let yourself go onto autopilot. Keep your speed down and drive slowly – let your braking, acceleration and steering all be gentle and unhurried. Keep your radio tuned to a local station as weather conditions can change quickly and they'll have the most up-to-date advice for motorists.

If you normally travel along country back lanes and it's been snowing then alter your route to travel along main roads if possible – they're more likely to have been gritted.

Fresh snow offers more grip than ice so try not to follow the tyre marks of the vehicle in front of you on the road – though if you're off-road then following behind would make more sense as you'll be able to judge the depth of snow. Having said that, going off-road in bad weather conditions isn't a good idea unless you're experienced with that type of motoring and have to do it as part of your job (you're a vet or a farmer in the Outer Hebrides, for example).

Heavy snowfall really isn't the time to have a gung-ho attitude towards 'road closed' signs – don't ignore them and decide to drive on anyway, even if you're in a 4x4 – not least because if you get lost or stuck then no one is going to go searching for you there.

Ice

Any driver with an ounce of sense knows they should drive carefully on icy roads. But when the day has warmed up and much of the ice seems to have melted, it's easy to get caught out – be aware that there can still be ice in places the sun hasn't been able to get to properly yet, such as under bridges or tree cover or where there are dips in the road. To be driving along at a normal speed and then unexpectedly find icy conditions below you can be alarming – stay calm though and avoid braking suddenly.

Black ice

Black ice is a nasty thing to have to deal with. It's formed when water on the road surface freezes and as it blends in with the dark colour of the tarmac it's much harder to spot than normal ice, which is pale and shiny. If you realize that the feel of the road beneath your tyres has suddenly changed, it's probably because you've hit a patch of black ice – again, stay calm and avoid sudden braking.

Think before you park

When you're parking up in wintry weather it's important to think ahead. If the conditions become more icy or there's a heavy snowfall, will you be able to pull away? Try to park facing downhill or on a level surface as driving off on an uphill slope is likely to prove risky.

Getting stuck in the snow

Returning to a snowed-in car can feel daunting. But as long as it's not too deep there are lots of little tricks for getting yourself out.

Clear away as much snow as you can from in front of the wheels with your shovel – if you haven't got one then improvise with anything handy – maybe the ice-scraper?

As mentioned earlier, cat litter is great for providing grip for your tyres – if you've got some in the boot now's the time to scatter it around. If you don't have any cat litter you're going to have to be resourceful in a Girl Guideish sort of way. Gather together some leaves, twigs, small stones or the footwell mats and put them around the tyres.

Start the engine and keep the car rocking between first gear and reverse – going forward and backwards as far as you can until you've built up the momentum to rock 'out and over' any snow that's built up around you.

Summer dreams

Summer driving can be a real pleasure – with the top down, the sunroof or even just the window open, cruising along can feel as though you're in a video for a summery pop song. But there are some things to bear in mind.

- ⊕ It's vital to have sunglasses in the car so you can protect yourself against the glare of the sun.
- ⊕ In heavy traffic it's especially important to keep your eye on the temperature gauge, as engines can easily overheat in these circumstances.
- ⊕ When you come back to the car on a hot day you might find the steering wheel has become really hot. One way of dealing with this is to invest in a steering wheel cover – they're not all pink and fluffy – there are some really nice ones at www.me-mo.co.uk, or you can get more sober versions at Halfords.

All year round

Rain

The usual rule for stopping distances is to leave a two-second gap between yourself and the car in front – but in wet weather you should increase it to four seconds. It's also a good idea to switch on your headlights in rainy weather. Rain is at its most dangerous after a prolonged dry spell as oil and grease will have built up over time and the addition of water can form oil slicks – so be aware of the danger of skidding.

And try not to splash pedestrians – it's bad karma.

Floods

Think very, very carefully before driving through a flood or a ford that's higher than usual. Maybe you're late, maybe it'll be a hassle to take another route – and yes, maybe other cars are making it through. But maybe yours won't. And the bill for repairing a flood-damaged engine can bring tears to your eyes, especially if it's a diesel.

If you do venture through, then always test your brakes afterwards to check they haven't been affected.

Fog

Fog can be spooky, scary stuff to drive in. One minute everything is perfectly clear, the next you're surrounded by an impenetrable blanket. It lifts and you assume everything is back to normal . . . and then you run straight into another patch. It's important to be alert in foggy conditions as they can be responsible for lots of accidents – nasty motorway pile-ups are often the result of fog. So you need to be prepared to deal with any problems ahead.

Put on your foglights and use dipped headlights – don't use full beam as the light will bounce off the fog and make the visibility even worse. Use your windscreen wipers to clear moisture from the windscreen – even if you don't need them on properly, do a flick-wipe every so often. Automatic windscreen wipers don't necessarily switch themselves on in fog as they don't always pick up on the fine mist, so be sure you know how to operate them manually. And of course slow your speed right down and be aware that pedestrians will be especially difficult to spot in these conditions.

Girls behaving badly

Getting a parking ticket

If you park illegally you'll probably get a parking ticket and have to pay a fine – though it can get a lot worse than that in some locations where clamping and towing are the parking punishments of choice. So check the road signs very carefully before leaving your car – and bear in mind that in some places signs can be ambiguous and poorly marked. If you're in any doubt at all it's best to move and find somewhere else to park.

If you do get fined it's best to just stump up and put it down to experience rather than turn into one of those people who gets all bitter and rants endlessly at the gross injustice. After all, the regulations are there for a purpose – for safety reasons, to ease congestion or to protect residents' parking rights. And it's worth remembering that parking in disabled spaces without a blue badge is particularly bad for your karma.

Talking on your mobile

The use of hand-held mobile phones was banned in December 2003 and if you're caught using one you'll get points on your licence. However, hands-free models can also have a negative effect on your driving as the conversation distracts you from what's happening on the road. So no matter how addicted you are to your mobile, turn it off when driving. There will never be a call or text message that's worth risking someone's life for.

Drinking and driving

Never mix alcohol and driving. Drink-driving can have tragic consequences. The Road Casualties Great Britain annual report 2004 published by the DfT revealed that 17 per cent of all fatal accidents involved drivers over the legal alcohol limit. And it's a problem that's getting worse – the numbers of people killed or injured by drink-drivers have both increased by over a third over the past decade. Even if you're not involved in an accident, the penalty for driving over the limit is automatic disqualification for at least a year, though this can be longer at the court's discretion. They are also allowed to impose a fine of up to £5000 and a prison sentence of up to six months.

So although taking a zero-tolerance approach might feel tough, it's actually much simpler – it means you don't have to end up worrying about the size of different measures or wondering, 'will I be all right with just a small glass?' The legal limit is a blood alcohol level of 80 mg/100 ml but even an amount well under that can affect your coordination and make accidents more likely. And staying 'under the limit' is a really tricky business. Different types of beers, wines and alcopops have varying strengths, the effect varies depending on your weight, metabolism, and whether you've eaten recently, and if you're at a party you'll probably be offered a drink that contains two or three times as much alcohol as you'd get in a pub measure.

Here are some tips for keeping your drinking and driving apart.

Do an analysis of your social life and work out the times when having a drink makes a real difference to your enjoyment and those when it wouldn't matter. For example, you might be happy to stick to soft drinks on a night out with your girlfriends, but really miss not being able to get a bit plastered at a party or gig. That way, you can drive some of the time and save your money for splashing out on taxis at other times. Track down some bars that serve smoothies, a variety of coffees or groovy non-alcoholic cocktails and arrange to meet your mates there on the nights you're avoiding the booze.

If you're on a weight-loss diet, remind yourself that alcohol tends to be high in calories and cutting back on it means more opportunity to indulge in chips or chocolate.

If you're the chauffeur for the evening and find yourself dourly surveying your mineral water or orange juice, feeling cheated and hard done by, promise yourself a winding-down glass of wine in front of some late-night junk TV when you get home.

Arranging a lift home from a non-drinking mate is great, but be aware that the situation might change. They might want to leave earlier or later than you, take a detour via some dubious-sounding party or their car might break down. They might decide to drink after all, and you could decide that you wouldn't feel safe being their passenger. Always have backup in the form of the number of a reliable cab firm and your fare home on you.

Better still, always have the numbers of several cab firms stored in your mobile – that way you've got a better chance of finding one that can pick you up fairly promptly.

If you stay somewhere overnight and plan to drive home in the morning, you need to be aware that, if you've drunk a lot, you may still be over the limit the following day. On average, it takes 1 hour per unit + 1 hour for alcohol to leave your system. So given that one unit of alcohol is a small pub measure (125 ml) of wine, if you've had two glasses it'll take three hours to leave your system, four glasses will take five hours and a bottle of wine (six 125 ml glasses) will take seven hours. If you're concerned that you might still be over the limit, take public transport home or into work, or have breakfast and go out for a walk until the alcohol has left your system.

Drugs

Hopefully you're not the sort of girl who would even consider taking hard drugs in the first place, let alone driving afterwards.

But it's important not even to be tempted to share a joint that's going around at a party – it'll slow your reactions and be highly dangerous once you're behind the wheel. Increasingly the police are taking blood and urine tests from drivers they suspect of being under the influence of drugs so don't think the fact you'd pass a breathalyser test will protect you from prosecution.

Losing your licence

Drivers who accumulate twelve or more penalty points on their licence over a three-year period will be disqualified from driving for a minimum of six months. And once you are allowed to drive again, you'll find that your car insurance premiums have rocketed.

New Drivers' Act – tremble before it!

The New Drivers' Act means that if you accumulate six or more penalty points during your first two years of driving, your licence will be revoked. You will then need to re-take both your theory and practical tests. Bearing in mind that you get a minimum of three penalty points for speeding, it only takes two such offences and you can say goodbye to your precious licence. Something to bear in mind when you're in a hurry and are tempted to push the speed limit or commit another driving offence.

The extended driving test – this is even worse!

If you're convicted of dangerous driving, you will lose your licence and after a period of disqualification may have to take an extended driving test in order to drive again. It's longer than the regular test (seventy minutes rather than forty) and more demanding.

Personal safety for girls on the go

Most women tend to feel much safer in their cars than they do using public transport. But don't let that make you complacent. Although road rage, car-jacking and being attacked when in or approaching your car are thankfully rare, it's wise to take simple precautions to keep yourself safe. The Suzy Lamplugh Trust (see reference section for details) has excellent advice on driving safely, but here are some basic guidelines:

- Always make sure your car is in good working order and there's no risk of running out of fuel.
- Always keep your doors locked when you're driving along.
- If someone in another car tries to attract your attention, ignore them and avoid making eye contact.

⊖ If you think you're being followed, drive to a police station or somewhere busy such as a pub or service station and phone for help from there.

⊖ Don't pick up hitchhikers.

⊖ Avoid 'road rage' situations – don't shout at or deliberately obstruct other drivers, and do your best to ignore it if they shout at or obstruct you.

⊖ If you see an accident or incident, think before you automatically stop to help. Ask yourself if it might be better to ring the police.

⊖ If a car pulls in front of you and forces you to stop, keep your engine running. Ensure your doors and windows are locked. If the driver leaves their car to approach you, try to reverse as far as possible and drive away. Put your hazard lights on and sound your horn as well.

Parking safely

Think ahead when you're parking – if you're parking in daylight but will return after dark, ask yourself what the area might be like then. If you think you might feel isolated or threatened then find somewhere else to park.

Reverse into parking bays, as it'll be easier to get away briskly.

If you're using a multi-storey car park and there's an attendant, try to park near his booth.

If possible, use a 'secured car park' – these are approved by the Association of Police Officers. To find one near you, look at www.securedcarparks.com.

Keep valuables out of sight and in particular don't let your car reveal that it belongs to a woman – keep heels, handbags, etc. out of sight.

Ask a friend or colleague to walk you to your car if you feel apprehensive.

When you return to your car, have your keys ready, check the back seat before you get in and then lock the doors immediately.

Some police authorities run short courses on coping with road rage and safe driving for women, which can be well worth attending.

Chapter 11

Baby, When You're at the Wheel

What with rising fuel prices, getting stuck in two-hour tail-backs, and concerns about your carbon footprint and road rage, it's easy to forget about the fun, life-enhancing aspects of motoring.

The next section is a celebration of all that's fantastic about motoring – from the most beautiful driving roads in the UK to music on the move and how to drive with the top down and still keep your hair looking great.

Driving with the top down

Driving with the top down can feel fantastic – but will it leave you looking as good as you feel? Here are some tips for avoiding mad, tangled hair and sunburned skin peeling off your nose.

- Sunscreen – unless you want a weatherbeaten Fisherman's Friend sort of complexion, a sunscreen with a high SPF is essential.
- Big shades – not only do they give you that essential Thelma and Louise glamour, they'll stop you from getting grit in your eyes or squinting so much that you get crow's feet. They also come in handy for helping you to look

aloof and ignore any unwanted suitors trying to chat you up at traffic lights.

⊕ Headgear – if you want to keep your hair looking good, a baseball cap will do for protection. But a wide head-band to keep your hair back will do the same job more stylishly. And to score top style points, go for retro chic with a Grace Kelly-inspired silk headscarf.

Music on the move

Built-in car radios date back to the 1930s and it's rare these days to find a car without a radio or CD player on the dash-board. And of course in recent years the introduction of MP3 players means that there's a whole new route to hearing your choice of music on the move.

The simplest way to connect your MP3 player to your car stereo is to use an FM transmitter. It'll connect to your MP3 player's headphone socket, then transmit its music on an FM signal. You can then tune your car's stereo into it.

If your car has an 'in-line' connection then there's the option of hooking up through that. It'll look like a headphone socket on the front and means you can connect your MP3 player's headphone socket using an audio cable.

If your car stereo is even more advanced, there could be a USB socket on the front. Use the USB cable that came with your MP3 player to hook it up directly. That'll mean you get full quality and your stereo will even display the names of the songs and let you control the music through it.

The UK's Favourite Driving Songs

From a survey by the insurance company Elephant

'Mr Brightside' – The Killers
'Holding Out for a Hero' – Bonnie Tyler
'In the Air Tonight' – Phil Collins
'American Pie' – Don McLean
'Paradise City' – Guns N' Roses
'Born to Be Wild' – Steppenwolf
'I Drove All Night' – Cyndi Lauper
'Eye of the Tiger' – Survivor
'Stuck in the Middle with You' – Stealers Wheel
'Mustang Sally' – Wilson Pickett

Whether you agree with these choices or are horrified by them and would prefer a bit of cool jazz or Gregorian chanting, there's no doubt that the right sort of music on the move can really enhance your driving experience.

Or then again, you could make your own . . .

A survey by Vauxhall Motors discovered that 87 per cent of us like to sing while driving. And in many ways, the car is the perfect place. If you're self-conscious about your voice then driving alone is the perfect opportunity to exercise your vocal cords –

no worries about unappreciative family, flatmates or neighbours wincing and sniggering at your attempt to hit those Christina Aguilera-style top notes.

Your voice is also going to sound better in the car, as the acoustics in the car will enhance it. The combination of sound-reflecting surfaces that support the quality and sound-absorbing surfaces which increase clarity will have you wondering if you've got that X-Factor potential.

To make it sound even better follow these tips:

Warm up with some deep breaths and warm-up exercises, for example 'me-me-me-me', up and down the scale.

Sit up straight with your chin up to keep your airways clear and project your voice.

Keep heating and air conditioning to a minimum as these can dry the throat.

Most beautiful driving roads

Seven best driving roads in Britain as voted by Caterham 7 sports car owners

- ☻ A87 Invergarry to the Isle of Skye – 'as breathtaking as it's challenging'.
- ☻ A4086 'Pass of Llanberis' from Caernarfon to Capel Curig, North Wales – 'popular destination, but twisty road and Snowdonia backdrop make it a must-drive'.
- ☻ A827 Killin to Ballinluig, Scotland – 'clear roads and just fun, fun, fun'.

- ☻ B4407 Ffestiniog to Pentrefoelas, North Wales – 'a demanding drive but clear views for miles'.
- ☻ A686 Penrith to Hayden Bridge through Gilderdale Forest, Pennines – 'English countryside at its finest'.
- ☻ B3223 across the Brendon Hills and Exmoor forest – 'narrow but flowing bends that beg to be driven'.
- ☻ B3306 St Just to St Ives, South West – 'can be busy with tourists but worth an early start any day'.

Driving cats and dogs

If you've got pets then there are times when you're going to have to transport them, whether that's to the vet, on holiday, or when you're moving house.

Dogs often like travelling – especially if they sense it might involve a long walk at some point.

Cats, on the other hand, generally hate it. 'I've known a few Siamese cats who enjoyed going in the car,' says David McDowell, veterinary expert at the RSPCA. 'But most cats are very unhappy in that environment, so it's important to keep the journeys to a minimum and do everything you can to make them as stress-free as possible.'

Dogs on the go

Traditionally, people have let dogs sit either on the back seat or beside them in the passenger seat – where sometimes they've even been allowed to stick their head out of the open window for the full 'wind in your hair' motoring experience.

But this really isn't a good idea. You wouldn't let a child lean out of the window like that because you'd be worried that they might get bumped by a passing vehicle or get grit or stones in their eyes – and so by the same principle you shouldn't let your dog do it either.

And with growing awareness of safety issues people are also realizing that dogs, like people, should have some sort of safety harness in the car. 'It's important to fit a harness so your dog doesn't end up going through the windscreen if you crash,' says Julie Bedford, animal behaviourist at the animal charity, the Blue Cross. 'A restraint also means that the dog won't get catapulted into you either, and if there's an accident then having it secured means it won't escape and run off into the traffic.'

One easy way you can do this is to invest in a dog seat belt. This is like a harness, padded on the chest and available in a range of sizes, which hooks onto the proper seat belt. It's a really simple and inexpensive way to keep your dog safe and you can buy them from any major pet store.

Another popular place for dogs to travel is in the back of the car. If you've got an estate car it's possible to get dog guards to put behind the back seat – the best ones are those made specifically for your make and model of vehicle. You should be able to find them on the website for your make of car.

Dog cages are a better and safer option. Made-to-measure cages are best but cheaper, ready-made ones are available from under £100 from the RAC website or from larger pet stores, which should have a range available. It's important to choose one that your dog can lie in comfortably.

Travelling longer distances

If you're travelling longer distances with your dog it's important to plan ahead. Exercise them well before you set off so they're tired already and are more likely to sleep on the journey.

Obviously you'll need to take water, and taking your local tap water is best as water smells different in different areas and having as many familiar things as possible will help keep stress levels down on a long journey.

It's important to keep an eye on how your dog is coping with the journey, particularly if they're travelling in the back of the car on a hot day. This is the part of the vehicle where the temperature is going to be highest, so although you might be fine, they could be really overheated and uncomfortable.

You should be stopping every couple of hours on a long journey anyway, to keep yourself alert and rested. This is especially important when you're travelling with your dog as they'll need to stretch their legs and relieve themselves (don't forget those necessary bags!). Lots of motorways have dog-friendly policies and if you want to find some good walks along the way check out the website www.walkingwithdogs.co.uk.

Never, never, never leave your dog in a hot car

You've heard it so many times, but it's really important not to. 'Leaving a window open or a water bowl in the car isn't good enough,' says Julie Bedford of the Blue Cross. 'When the sun is shining at virtually any time of year, the inside of the car can quickly become far too hot and dangerous for your pet.'

Dogs that don't like the car

If your dog hates going in the car or gets car-sick, then driving as smoothly as possible may well improve matters. And experiment with letting your dog travel in different parts of the car – ones that aren't happy in the back may well do fine in the front and vice versa.

Another useful tactic is to get your dog used to short journeys first – maybe put it in the car to just travel 300 yards to do its favourite walk, so it starts to see the car in a more positive light.

If the problem persists, then ask your vet to recommend an animal behaviourist who will help you get to the root of the problem.

Cool for cats

Most cats dislike travelling, so keep any journeys in the car to a minimum. Most can just about manage travelling a short distance to the vet or cattery but as most people who've ever had to move a cat long distances will know, it can really upset them.

> *My cat Midge hates travelling. She mews in distress all the time and often throws up as well. It makes me feel so guilty and stressed as I'm driving along. The worst time was when I was moving house from London to Devon. It was such a long journey that she ended up in a terrible state. And then just as I thought it couldn't get any worse, we got caught up in holiday traffic and she started pooing! There was no way I could deal with it as we were stuck in a traffic jam – so I was sitting there bumper to bumper with other cars on a hot day in a car that smelt of cat poo. I swear I'll never move house again! Jessie, 27*

Under no circumstances let your cat loose in the car. It must be in a closed cat basket or cage – all major pet shops have a good selection for you to choose from, and you can fasten a seat belt around it to keep it secure.

'I've found that cats tend to be happier if they can look out,' says vet David McDowell. 'So I'd advise a basket with a wire grille at the front.' It can be a good idea to introduce the travel basket to the cat in advance – maybe near a favourite sleeping place such as the conservatory or a radiator so that they become familiar with it. Putting in bedding that smells of you, such as an old vest, can be comforting to your pet. Offer food, water and a litter tray on long journeys, though it's likely that your cat will be very withdrawn and not want anything to do with them. And if your cat really hates travelling and you've got no option but to take her on a long journey, then it might be worth visiting your vet to see if she could be prescribed a sedative.

For more information, RoSPA has a leaflet on 'Carrying Pets Safely' which can be downloaded at www.rospa.com.

Chapter 12

Are We There Yet?

Car seats

Parenting isn't exactly short of challenges – and fitting car seats and strapping your children into them has got to be up there with getting them to eat broccoli as one of the front-runners.

It took me ages to get the hang of the car seat – first you have to fit them, then you have to work out how to strap the children in. Nobody warns you that when you become a parent you need a degree in mechanical engineering. Or is it just my ineptitude? Apart from the technicalities, strapping a small child into a car seat when they don't want to be can be a nightmare. I once hurt my back when leaning over to strap my daughter into the seat, and the osteopath said that he saw that sort of back injury all the time. Clare, 32

When my daughter doesn't want to get into her car seat, she puffs her chest out so she is curved away from the chair. I lengthen the straps, do them up and pull them gradually tighter so she has to wiggle back. Blowing a raspberry on her tummy sometimes works because it makes her giggle and sit back. Camilla, 37

But car seats are non-negotiable – for both parents and children. Persuading reluctant children to stay meekly strapped in them can be difficult, but it can be done.

When my eldest daughter Hayley was two she started taking off her car seat straps as I was driving. I stopped the first time and told her I wouldn't move until she put them back on. As it continued I decided to make a specific car journey for no reason other than to teach her to keep them on. We stopped every time she took them off and sat in silence until she got the message. I didn't have to rush anywhere as there was no other purpose to the journey and she soon got bored. Kitty, 26

It's vital that babies and children should be strapped into a suitable child restraint when in the car – don't be tempted to carry them in your arms, not even for short journeys. Adult seat belts aren't suitable for children as they're designed for much larger people and in a crash a child might slide under an adult belt because the lap strap is too high over their abdomen, or it could cause internal injuries.

If you're transporting other people's children then you're legally responsible for ensuring that they're in a suitable seat. Failure to comply with these laws can result in a £30 fixed penalty fine or a fine of up to £500 if the case goes to court.

There are lots of options to choose from but it's very important to install them properly. Some stores, such as John Lewis and certain branches of Mothercare and Halfords, have trained staff who can demonstrate how to fit them, so it's best to buy from one of those stores if at all possible. Don't be tempted to buy one second-hand as it might have been involved in an accident, have missing parts or not come with the full instructions.

New cars are now built with ISOFix points built into them. ISOFix stands for International Standards Organisation Fix and was developed to make fitting car seats safer and easier. It involves having set fitting points for the car seat actually built into the car itself and is safer and more reliable than the old method, whereby the car seat is attached using the adult seat belt. However, not every ISOFix seat will fit every car, so make sure the one you're considering is suitable for your particular make and model before buying it.

Guidelines for car seats are very individual – they'll depend on the age, weight and height of the particular child. You'll find detailed information on the Royal Society for the Prevention of Accidents (RoSPA) website – www.rospa.com. Also contact your local road safety unit, which may have an advice, fitting and checking service. Here are some general guidelines.

Baby seat

These are for babies, from newborns to at least one-year-olds, and often convert to carriers when removed from the car. It's best to check out baby seats before the baby is born – then at least that's one less thing to arrange!

Child safety seat

These start with ones aimed at toddlers. The safest arrangement is to have them facing the rear for as long as possible – until they've outgrown the position. Then it's time to move them to a front-facing child seat.

Booster seat

Booster seats are used after child safety seats and before the rite of passage that is using the car's actual seat belt. The child should be at least three years old before attempting to use a booster seat.

Travelling with children

When it comes to travelling with children, planning is everything. The more you think ahead about food and drink, sleep patterns, entertainment, nappy changing and trips to the loo, the easier things will be. Here are some tips from the parenting front line.

Food and drink

It's best just to have water in the car – but if you do have juice or fizzy drinks it's advisable to go for cartons with spouts or children's flasks rather than normal bottles or cans. Avoid messy food like chocolate or oranges and substitute chewy sweets or apple slices.

Comfort breaks

Children vary in how often they need to go to the loo. It's best always to ask as you're approaching a service station.

> *When my daughter was younger she did have a phase of always needing to go to the toilet when we were on the M25 without a service stop for another thirty miles, but this was so awful I am trying to blot it out of my memory.* Annabel, 40

Sunshades

On hot days protect your child from the heat and glare by using an adjustable sunshade that you can move to different windows as the sun moves.

Spare change of clothes

It's good to always have a change of clothes in the boot, even if they're well beyond the potty-training stage as it makes spillages and episodes of car-sickness so much less stressful.

It's possible to buy a rearward-facing mirror so you can keep an eye on the children behind you, whether that's watching out for signs of imminent car-sickness or nipping any fights in the bud – though of course it's important not to get too drawn into back-seat dramas at the expense of what's happening on the road!

But no matter how good your planning, there are going to be times when everything goes very badly wrong – and you're just going to have to be philosophical about it.

> *I well remember being in a traffic jam on the M6 when my daughter was about three months old and it took me twenty minutes to drive three miles to the next service station with her screaming the entire way because she was hungry. By the time we got there my shirt was drenched with milk (gross) and she was covered in sweat and had turned a really alarming shade of red, presumably through outrage at the whole situation.*
> Samantha, 30

The school run

If you live near your children's school then it's worth considering whether it might be possible to free yourself from the tyranny of the school run. Maybe you could walk them there, or, depending on their age, they might be able to travel with other children, walk or cycle there themselves. The website www.school-run.org can put you in touch with other parents with whom to share the school run, whether by car, bike or on foot. There are more tips on this in Chapter 13, 'Greener Motoring'.

When you are driving your children to school allow plenty of time for the journey. Make sure you have a policy that any books, sports equipment and so on has to be taken with you to the car and that you're not going back for anything under any circumstances. Drive within the speed limit (no matter how late you are!) and park considerately, without blocking driveways. Don't stop on the yellow zig-zags, not even briefly, and always ensure that children get out on the pavement side.

If any arguments kick off on the journey to school don't get involved in them – say that you'll talk about it that evening, when you're at home. Rows can seriously distract everyone and make for dangerous driving. Remember that if you want your children to go on to be safe drivers themselves it's important to lead by example – if they see you being a short-tempered speed freak they're more likely to be like that themselves in years to come.

The school disco run

Picture the scene. You've had a hard week at work and all that's keeping you going is the thought of staggering through the front door – slinging supper together and pouring yourself a nice cool glass of Chardonnay. And then getting quietly sloshed in front of your favourite TV programme. Except that you, er, can't because you're expected to pick up teenage Joshua or Tamsin from their school disco or party at their friend's house – which doesn't finish until 11 p.m.!

One of the advantages of ballet and scouts is at least they finish reasonably early – you can be back home by 9 p.m. at the latest. But late nights at friends' houses – whether it's having a party or just 'hanging out' – can go on till midnight or beyond. It's a tricky stage – when your children are old enough to want to stay out late but not old enough to drive themselves or use public transport after a certain time.

> *I find it really difficult. At the end of a busy week I want to unwind but instead I'm left sitting bolt upright at 11 p.m., sober as a judge, and irritably jangling my car keys and getting ready to pick my son up from a party at his friend's house. I don't even have the option of binge-drinking the alcohol I would normally have consumed over the length of the evening when I get back because I've got to get up at 7 a.m. the next morning to drive my daughter to a netball tournament.* Julia, 55

There are a number of possible solutions, though many of them will be dependent on family support, finances and other factors.

Maybe you and your partner could take it in turns to pick them up – or if there's a responsible, old-enough-to-drive sibling at home perhaps they could pitch in occasionally. Arrange lift-sharing among other families in the same boat. Try tracking down a trustworthy cab firm – if you book early enough, you may be able to stipulate a female driver.

Long journeys

If you're planning a long journey with your family, it's important to consider when will be the best time to set off. Some parents swear by the 'driving through the night' strategy. But before you go for this one, bear in mind that although the children will be tired, you will be too and you'll have to wake them up at the other end.

Other options include going after breakfast, or just after lunch when they've had the morning to play and hopefully will have a bit of an afternoon nap.

It's also worth considering whether it might be a good idea to take a different route from the one you would if you were travelling alone – for example instead of going on the motorway, you could plump for A-roads where it's easier to stop.

When I drive down to Devon to see my family I always take the A303 rather than the motorway. It's easier to pull over if necessary. Like when my children urgently cry out, 'Stop, Mummy, stop the car!' and I'll drive into a lay-by, turn round to see what disaster has taken place only to be instructed to, 'Sing a song, Mummy, sing a song!'
Ellen, 31

Car-sickness

Some children suffer terribly from car-sickness. This is where having seat covers and a spare change of clothes comes in really useful!

To avoid car-sickness, keep your driving as smooth as possible and allow plenty of fresh air into the car. Games that involve looking out of the window can be particularly useful in fending off car-sickness. Keep the children's meals on the journey light and healthy – salads rather than burgers or fry-ups.

Reading can make matters worse, so it's better to have story tapes on.

Ginger and peppermint both have good reputations for preventing car-sickness – you can buy capsules and tinctures in health food shops. It's important to take it in advance as car-sickness can be difficult to stop once it's started.

If the worst comes to the worst, there's advice on dealing with the consequences in Chapter 3, 'How Clean Is Your Car?'.

Regular stops

It's important to allow time in your journey for frequent stops when you're travelling with young children – not just for toilet breaks and nappy changes, but to give toddlers and others the chance to run about and stretch their legs. Some motorway service stations have play areas, so do a bit of research beforehand and arrange to stop at one of those.

Mum, I'm bored!

Long journeys are dull enough for adults so it's not surprising that children can get bored and irritable. Driving at times when they're likely to be sleepy is ideal, but here are some ideas for when they're not.

DVDs, story tapes, iPods and PlayStations

Almost all parents sing the praises of modern in-car technology for keeping their children happy on long journeys. There is of course a slight feeling that maybe this is copping out and you all ought to be singing songs or playing I-Spy and generally bonding as a family in a wholesome 1950s sort of way.

But the fact is that older children would be horrified at the very thought of playing games together, and with the younger ones you can alternate between spells of interacting together and times when you let them slump, boggle-eyed, staring at a DVD screen or fiddling with their PlayStations.

> *My husband and I grit our teeth and put up with the kids' CDs and DVDs on long journeys – Kylie,* High School Musical *and so on. In-car DVDs are a godsend for long journeys, even though I do now know every word of* Pirates of the Caribbean *1 and 2.* Becky, 42

If you're going to use DVDs it's best to go for ones with earphones so it doesn't distract the driver. However, some parents are less than thrilled at the prospect of having a driving sound-track of children's songs or stories and take steps to convert them to their own choices.

> *I've never played children's CDs when driving – I'm trying to keep them from working out that having 'their music' in the car is possible for as long as I can. Right now they're into Bowie, Blondie and Nirvana.* Kitty, 26

Educational activities
Teaching them their times tables, the alphabet, historical dates and so on means the time can be spent productively – and leave more time over for playing at other times. If you're going abroad, learning some foreign phrases can be good fun!

Map-reading
Older children and teenagers can get really into map-reading, so get them to help you out with navigation.

Toys
Books are great – though best avoided if the child has a tendency towards car-sickness as it can make matters worse. Colouring books, puzzles, games and cards are also good. It's wise not to produce all the toys at once – dole them out gradually over the length of the journey so they've got novelty value.

It's great if you're ferrying children of similar age and interests, because they can play and chat together. But if you can come up with any ways to encourage agreeable interaction between siblings, then that's great.

If possible it's a good idea to attach books and toys to the car seat so they can't fall down out of reach of the child.

> *I've gradually amassed a toy bag containing an array of small toys to keep peace and quiet in the car: in fact, when the baby was too small*

to reach the toy bag, it was a nice role for the older child to be given the job of choosing and passing toys to the baby. Samantha, 30

Car games
Car games can actually be really good fun as long as you do them in short bursts and don't expect the same level of enthusiasm for the whole length of an eight-hour drive to Cornwall.

Last letter
A round-robin game. First choose a category – for example, animals, TV programmes, or countries. Then each player must suggest a word in that category from the last letter of the previous word. So if 'dog' was the opener, then the next player could go for 'giraffe'. If you can't think of one you're eliminated, and the winner is the last person left.

Pub cricket
You can't play it on the motorway, but it's good if you're going through towns and villages. Form two teams – one team takes the left-hand side of the road, the other the right-hand side. For each side, score one run for every foot or paw implied in the name – up to a maximum of six – so (for instance) a Queen Victoria scores two, a 'Dog and Duck' scores six. Lose a wicket for each name with no foot or paws – for example, 'The Rising Sun'. The game stops when one team has lost ten wickets. The winning team is the one with the most runs at that point.

Twenty questions
One player thinks of a famous person, place or thing. Everyone else is allowed to ask that player twenty questions, which can only be answered 'yes' or 'no'. Whoever guesses correctly gets a turn to think up the next challenge.

Driving bingo

Every player gets a type of bingo sheet with words describing the sort of things that might be seen on the journey – pub, church, river, tractor, monument, etc. The first person to tick all the words wins.

Number-plate numbers

A simple addition game where one player shouts out the numbers on a passing number-plate and the others add them up. The winner is the player who's given the most correct answers, quickest, by the end of the journey.

I-Spy

You've got to have a few rounds of I-Spy on a long family car journey – it's as traditional as reading out awful cracker jokes over Christmas dinner.

And finally, a perennial favourite with parents:

The quiet game

A prize for whoever can stay quiet the longest!

Chapter 13

Greener Motoring

Greener motoring sounds like a good idea. After all, most of us are keen to stop the ice-floes melting, save polar bears and so on. But it doesn't always feel that easy to put into practice.

At home, it's so much more straightforward. You put your newspapers and plastic bottles in the relevant recycling containers. You turn off electrical appliances rather than keeping them on standby. Job done. But one of the main tenets of greener motoring does involve using the car less and walking more – which many of us aren't that enthusiastic about.

People use cars when they shouldn't – me included. But I always have an excuse – I'm in a hurry, it's raining, I have too much to carry. I have an excuse for every occasion! Laura, 24

And there's also the fact that a lot of the information that's put out about greener motoring seems so complicated – and often contradictory. For example, at one moment cars like the Toyota Prius are being hailed as the new face of eco-motoring, the next they're being criticized because they take so much energy to make. Then the tree-huggy-sounding biofuels are seen as the answer. Until someone mentions that their production involves taking up land that should be used for growing food.

In short, there are a lot of myths and misunderstandings about greener motoring and having a grasp of the facts behind them will make it easier for you to work out how you can do your bit.

Different sorts of fuel

Concerns about global warming mean that the debate about 'greener motoring' tends to focus on CO_2 emissions and side-step the fact that all the energy sources currently used to power our cars have some downsides. Here's a roundup of what we're using:

Petrol and diesel (fossil fuels)

When these are used they give off CO_2 into the atmosphere, contributing towards greenhouse gases, the hole in the ozone layer and all sorts of bad stuff like that.

Biofuels

These include biodiesel and bioethanol. These fuels are made from plant materials, and although they give off CO_2 when they are burnt, the plants also absorbed it quite recently from the atmosphere as they were growing, so a balance is maintained. However, fossil fuels were laid down millions of years ago so burning them and releasing their CO_2 puts everything severely out of kilter and contributes towards global warming.

Electricity

So-called 'hybrid' cars, like the Toyota Prius, use a mixture of fossil fuels and electricity. And electric cars like the G-Wiz are powered purely by electricity. However, the electrical energy has to come from somewhere – and that's generally nuclear power stations, which don't have a huge fan club among committed environmentalists either.

> *I think 'green driving' is currently causing as many problems as it aims to solve. Driving isn't green and never will be until we find a genuinely eco-logically friendly fuel. Biofuels are not the answer – thousands of acres previously used to grow food crops are now being turned over to fuel crops with resulting food shortages for the local people. And then there's all this fuss about hybrid and electric cars – but then, where's the energy to run them going to come from? At the moment the answer seems to be nuclear power stations – and they're not without their problems, either!* Jessie, 27

Green motoring – your questions answered!

How about I just drive my 4x4 everywhere and then pay a carbon offsetting scheme to plant a few trees or something?

It's not as simple as that, unfortunately. 'Offsetting schemes are a smokescreen,' says Tony Bosworth of Friends of the Earth.

They're used a lot by the aviation industry – there are lots of websites that will calculate what you've used by flying and offer to invest in tree planting to make up for the CO2 you've used. But there are real doubts about the validity of some of the schemes at the moment. We're currently investigating to see which, if any, we could recommend.

And while we're on the subject of 4x4s – are they really the work of Satan?

Most 4x4s are big, heavy cars – and that's why they need powerful engines and lots of fuel to be hauled around. However, some aren't as bad as you might expect – for example, the Honda CR-V doesn't actually produce any more CO2 than a typical family estate car. And Land Rover is currently working on a diesel hybrid prototype – if they get it right, it could be hailed as a green version of the 4x4.

Should I change my car for a newer, greener one?

The emphasis on 'greener motoring' always seems to be on new developments – hybrids like the Toyota Prius, electric cars like the G-Wiz – and the motoring press is forever scanning the horizon for the Next Big Thing.

But in fact, so much energy has to go into manufacturing new cars that a well-maintained older car can be just as good for keeping CO2 emissions down as one of the cutting-edge newer models.

How can I find the greenest car for me?

Go to the website of the Environmental Transport Association, www.eta.co.uk, or www.whatgreencar.com. You can type in what sort of car you're looking for – from a small city car to a large family estate or even a sporty number – and it will give you a selection to choose from.

Fuel-efficient driving

You can cut your fuel consumption 8.5 per cent on average by driving in the right way. And, as was pointed out in Chapter 2, 'Money and Your Motor', even if you don't have naturally green inclinations, it'll be good for your finances.

- ⌖ Care for your car – getting it serviced regularly will help keep its fuel economy as good as possible.
- ⌖ Under pressure – getting your tyre pressure correct is one of the most effective steps you can take for keeping your consumption down.
- ⌖ Plan your journey – by planning the best route for your journey in advance you'll save time and fuel – trying to travel out of rush hour helps you avoid congestion.
- ⌖ Avoid short journeys – pollution is worse when the engine is cold. It takes at least a mile to warm up, so it's a good idea to walk or cycle on shorter trips.
- ⌖ Easy driver – fast accelerating and harsh braking uses up fuel like nobody's business. Driving smoothly will keep consumption as low as possible.
- ⌖ Don't idle – switch off your engine if you expect to be stationary for more than a minute.

- ⊕ Slower is greener – the faster you go, the more fuel you burn. For example, cruising at 80 m.p.h. you'll use around 20 per cent more fuel than at 70 m.p.h. (the legal limit). So you'll be saving on more than speeding fines!
- ⊕ Travel light – keep your boot free of non-essential items to reduce weight and thus reduce fuel consumption.
- ⊕ Go with the flow – the smoother the flow of air around your car, the less resistance there will be. So remove roof/bike racks when you're not using them (a full roof rack increases fuel consumption by 30 per cent and even an empty one will cause extra drag).

Reducing your car use

The most straightforward way to reduce your car use is to walk, cycle or take public transport more.

Car-sharing is also a growth area – particularly for commuting into work. Check out www.nationalcarshare.co.uk, the UK's longest-established national car-sharing service, for advice on how to hook up with likely sharers.

Car clubs are a really promising development. The idea is that you can hire one of their cars for any period of time – from an hour to a month. The car can be booked online or by phone, then you collect it from a pre-arranged parking place. It is unlocked with a smart card and pin number – and off you go!

The charges are based on how long you have the car and how far you drive – it's a bit like a pay-as-you go mobile phone and could be an excellent option, especially if you live in a major city where it's easy to get to your nearest club car.

I joined a car club after seeing the film, An Inconvenient Truth, *about global warming. Getting rid of my car was really scary, but now I always think 'bike first' when I'm considering going anywhere. The car club is a useful backup when I want to go to parties or arts events in the local countryside. One positive change is that I use nearby shops now rather than going to the supermarket and I feel a lot more connected to my local community.* Fiona, 42

Reference
Section

Driving organizations

Driver and Vehicle Licensing Agency (DVLA)
Customer Enquiries
Swansea
SA6 7JL
Tel: 0870 240 0009
www.dvla.gov.uk

For information on driving abroad, road tax and consumer advice and other motoring matters.

www.direct.gov.uk/motoring – The main government online motoring site, providing advice and links to online facilities for application and renewals.

Money and your motor

www.moneysavingexpert.com – A very helpful site run by financial journalist Martin Lewis which will have news of the best and most up-to-date deals for car insurance, fuel and breakdown cover. You'll also get excellent advice from posters on the very active forums.

www.petrolprices.com – Sign up and you'll be sent regular emails with news of the cheapest fuel prices in your area.

Caring for your car

The Motor Industry Code of Practice for Service and Repair

This scheme was launched in 2008 and garages who have signed up to it have agreed to high standards. There's also a free advice line if you run into problems with a garage that is a member of the scheme. A useful tool for finding a good garage in your area.

Tel: 0800 692 0825

www.motorindustrycodes.co.uk

Foxy Lady Drivers

A club giving advice and arranging special discounts for its female membership.

Tel: 01903 879988

www.foxyladydrivers.com

Buying a car

What Car? **magazine** – Clear and jargon-free, this is a great magazine to flick through when dreaming of your next car.

www.whatcar.com – The site linked to *What Car?* magazine with up-to-date and detailed car reviews. **www.evecars.com** is the women's version of the site.

www.honestjohn.co.uk – New- and used-car reviews written by a man who really knows his stuff.

www.autotrader.co.uk and **www.parkers.co.uk** – For details of cars available in your area, and an online facility for finding out how much your own might be worth in a private sale or dealer trade-in.

Beautifying your car

www.me-mo.co.uk – This fab car accessories site is the place to go for funky car seats and steering wheel covers, car boot organizers and – of course – pink fluffy dice!

Other useful organizations

**Royal Society for the Prevention
of Accidents (RoSPA)**
RoSPA House
Edgbaston Park
353 Bristol Road
Edgbaston
Birmingham
B5 7ST
Tel: 0121 248 2000
www.rospa.com

The website has useful leaflets available for downloading, including ones on driving during pregnancy, fitting safe child seats, advice on driving at night and winter driving.

The Suzy Lamplugh Trust
National Centre for Personal Safety
Hampton House
20 Albert Embankment
London
SE1 7TJ
Tel: 020 7091 0014
www.suzylamplugh.org.uk

This charity offers information on safety to both men and women. They have useful advice on staying safe in your car available both on their website and in a variety of leaflets. They also run courses on personal safety.

Institute of Advanced Motorists
IAM House
510 Chiswick High Road
London
W4 5RG
020 8996 9600
www.iam.org.uk

Index

NOTE ON THE AUTHOR

Maria McCarthy is a member of the Guild of Motoring Writers and has contributed to *Cosmopolitan*, the *Independent*, the *Guardian*, the *Sunday Express* and *MSN Cars*. She's also a popular media commentator on motoring matters and has appeared on *BBC Breakfast* news and Radio 5 Live. She is the author of *The Girls' Guide to Losing Your L-Plates: How to Pass Your Driving Test* and teaches Freelance Journalism and Path to Publication workshops at Bristol University. For more information see www.mariamccarthy.co.uk.